EDWARD ALBEE'S

TINY ALICE.

★

★

DRAMATISTS
PLAY SERVICE
INC.

For

NOEL FARRAND

EDWARD ALBEE

Mr. Albee was born March 12, 1928, and began writing plays thirty years later. His plays are in order of composition, The Zoo Story (1958); The Death of Bessie Smith (1959); The Sandbox (1959); The American Dream (1960); Who's Afraid of Virginia Woolf? (1961-1962); The Ballad of the Sad Café, *an adaptation of Carson Mc-Cullers' novella* (1963); *and* Tiny Alice (1964). *He is presently at work on a play entitled* The Substitute Speaker.

AUTHOR'S NOTE

It has been the expressed hope of many that I would write a preface to the published text of *Tiny Alice*, clarifying obscure points in the play—explaining my intention, in other words. I have decided against creating such a guide because I find—after reading the play over—that I share the view of even more people: that the play is quite clear. I will confess, though, that *Tiny Alice* is less opaque in reading than it would be in any single viewing. One further note: this printed text of *Tiny Alice* represents the complete play. Some deletions—mainly in the final act—were made for the New York production; and while I made the deletions myself, and quite cheerfully, realizing their wisdom in the particular situation, I restore them here with even greater enthusiasm.

EDWARD ALBEE

TINY ALICE was first presented by Theater 1965, Richard Barr and Clinton Wilder, at the Billy Rose Theatre, in New York City, on December 29, 1964. It was directed by Alan Schneider; William Ritman was the designer; the lighting was by Martin Aronstein; and gowns were by Mainbocher. The cast, in order of appearance, was as follows:

LAWYER .... William Hutt

CARDINAL .... Eric Berry

JULIAN .... John Gielgud

BUTLER .... John Heffernan

MISS ALICE .... Irene Worth

TINY ALICE

ACT I

SCENE 1

The Cardinal's garden. What is needed . . . ? Ivy climbing a partial wall of huge stones? An iron gate? Certainly two chairs—one, the larger, obviously for His Eminence, the other, smaller—and certainly an elaborate birdcage, to stage L., with some foliage in it, and two birds, cardinals . . . which need not be real.

AT RISE: *The Laywer is at the birdcage, talking to the birds.*

LAWYER. (*His back to audience.*) Oomm, yoom, yoom, um? Tick-tick-tick-tick-tick. Um? You do-do-do-do-do-um? Tick-tick-tick-tick-tick-tick-tick-um? (*He raises his fingers to the bars.*) Do-do-do-do-do-do-do? Aaaaaawwwww! Oomm, yoom, yoom, um? (*The Cardinal enters from R.—through the iron gates?—unseen by the Lawyer, who repeats some of the above as the Cardinal moves toward C.*)

CARDINAL. (*Finally. Quietly amused.*) Saint Francis?

LAWYER. (*Swinging around, flustered, perhaps more annoyed than embarrassed at being discovered.*) Your Eminence!

CARDINAL. (*Crosses in to C.*) Our dear Saint Francis, who wandered in the fields and forests, talked to all the . . .

LAWYER. (*Crosses R. to Cardinal, moves to kiss the ring.*) Your Eminence, we appreciate your kindness in taking the time to see us; we know how heavy a schedule you . . .

CARDINAL. (*Silencing him by waving his ring at him. The Lawyer kneels, kisses the ring.*) We are pleased . . . (*Cardinal crosses R. to R. chair. Lawyer rises.*) we are pleased to be your servant (*Trailing off.*) . . . if . . . we can be your servant. We addressed you as Saint Francis . . .

LAWYER. (*Properly mumbling.*) Oh, but surely . . .

7

CARDINAL. . . . as Saint Francis . . . who did talk to the birds so, did he not. And here we find *you*, who talk not only to the birds but to (*With a wave at the cage.*) —you must forgive us —to cardinals as well. (*Waits for reaction, gets none, tries again.*) . . . To cardinals? As well?

LAWYER. (*A tight smile.*) We . . . we understood.

CARDINAL. (*He, too. Cardinal sits in* R. *chair.*) Did we. (*A brief silence, as both smiles hold.*)

LAWYER. (*To break it, moving back* L. *toward the cage.*) We find it droll—if altogether appropriate in this setting—that there should be two cardinals . . . uh, together . . . (*Almost a sneer. Turns in to* C.) . . . in conversation, as it were.

CARDINAL. (*The smile again.*) Ah, well, they are a comfort to each other . . . companionship. And they have so much to say. They . . . understand each other so much better than they would . . . uh, *other* birds.

LAWYER. Indeed. And so much better than they would understand saints?

CARDINAL. (*Daring him to repeat it, but still amused.*) Sir?

LAWYER. (*Right in. Crosses* R. *to* C.) That cardinals understand each *other* better than they understand saints.

CARDINAL. (*Not rising to it.*) Who is to say? Will you sit?

LAWYER. (*Turns* L., *steps* L. *Peering into the cage.*) They are extraordinary birds . . . cardinals, if I may say so. . . .

CARDINAL. (*Through with it.*) You push it too far, sir. Will you join us?

LAWYER. (*Brief pause, then surrender, moves to the* L. *chair, sits.*) Of course.

CARDINAL. (*A deep sigh.*) Well. What should we do now? (*Pause.*) Should we clap our hands (*Does so, twice.*) . . . twice, and have a monk appear? A very old monk? With just a ring of white hair around the base of his head, stooped, fast-shuffling, his hands deep in his sleeves? Eh? And should we send him for wine? Um? Should we offer you wine, and should we send him scurrying off after it? Yes? Is that the scene you expect now?

LAWYER. (*Very relaxed, but pointed.*) It's so difficult to know what to expect in a Cardinal's garden, Your Eminence. An old monk would do . . . or—who is to say?— (*Looks off* R.) perhaps some good-looking young novice, all freshly scrubbed, with big working-class hands, who would . . .

CARDINAL. (*Magnanimous.*) We have both in our service; if a boy is more to your pleasure . . .

LAWYER. I don't drink in the afternoon, so there is need for neither . . . unless Your Eminence . . . ?

CARDINAL. (*His eyes sparkling with the joke to come about his nature.*) We are known to be . . . ascetic, so we will have none of it. Just . . . three cardinals . . . and Saint Francis.

LAWYER. Oh, not Saint Francis, not a saint. Closer to a king; closer to Croesus. (*Takes out cigarettes.*) That was gibberish I was speaking to the cardinals—and it's certainly not accepted that Saint Francis spoke gibberish to his . . . parishioners . . . intentional gibberish or otherwise.

CARDINAL. It is not accepted; no.

LAWYER. No. (*Lights cigarette.*) May I smoke?

CARDINAL. Do.

LAWYER. Closer to Croesus; to gold; closer to wealth.

CARDINAL. (*A heavy, weary sigh.*) Aahhhh, you *do* want to talk business, don't you?

LAWYER. (*Surprisingly tough.*) Oh, come on, Your Eminence: (*Softer.*) Do you want to spend the afternoon with me, making small talk? Shall we . . . shall we talk about . . . times gone by?

CARDINAL. (*Thinks about it with some distaste.*) No. No no; we don't think so. It wouldn't do. It's not charitable of us to say so, but when we were at school we did loathe you so. (*Both laugh slightly.*)

LAWYER. Your Eminence was not . . . beloved of everyone himself.

CARDINAL. (*Thinking back, a bit smugly.*) Ah, no; a bit out of place; out of step.

LAWYER. A swine, I thought. (*Looks at Cardinal.*)

CARDINAL. (*Looks at Lawyer.*) And we you. (*Both laugh a little again.*)

LAWYER. Do you ever slip?

CARDINAL. Sir?

LAWYER. Mightn't you—if you're not careful— (*Tiny pause.*) lapse . . . and say *I* to me . . . not we?

CARDINAL. (*Pretending sudden understanding.*) Ah ha! Yes, we understand.

LAWYER. Do we, do we.

CARDINAL. We do. We—and here we speak of our*selves* and

9

not of our station—we . . . *we* reserve the first-person singular for intimates . . . and equals.

LAWYER. . . . And your superiors.

CARDINAL. (*Brushing away a gnat.*) The case does not apply.

LAWYER. (*Matter-of-factly, the vengeance is underneath. Rises, crosses R. to D. of fountain.*) You'll grovel, Buddy. (*Slaps his hip hard.*) As automatically and naturally as people slobber on that ring of yours. (*Flicks cigarette ash in fountain.*) As naturally as that, I'll have you do your obeisance. (*Turns L. to Cardinal. Sweetly.*) As you used to, old friend.

CARDINAL. We . . . (*Thinks better of what he was about to say.*) You *were* a swine at school. (*More matter-of-factly.*) A cheat in your examinations, a liar in all things of any matter, vile in your personal habits—unwashed and indecent, a bully to those you could intimidate and a sycophant to everyone else. We remember you more clearly each moment. It is law you practice, is it not? We find it fitting.

LAWYER. (*A mock bow, head only.*) We are of the same school, Your Eminence.

CARDINAL. And in the same class . . . but not *of*. You have come far—in a worldly sense . . . from so little, we mean. (*Musing.*) The law.

LAWYER. I speak plainly.

CARDINAL. You are plain. As from your beginnings.

LAWYER. (*Crosses slowly L. to C. Quietly.*) Overstuffed, arrogant, pompous son of a profiteer. And a whore. You are in the Church, are you not? We find it fitting.

CARDINAL. (*A burst of appreciative laughter.*) You're good! You *are*! Still! Gutter, but good. But, in law . . . (*Leaves it unfinished with a gesture.*) Ah! It comes back to us; it begins to. What did we call you at school? (*Lawyer crosses U. into alcove.*) What name, what nickname did we have for you . . . all of us? What term of simple honesty and . . . rough affection did we have for you? (*Tapping his head impatiently.*) It comes back to us.

LAWYER. (*Almost a snarl.*) We had a name for you, too.

CARDINAL. (*Dismissing it.*) Yes, yes, but we forget it.

LAWYER. (*Crosses D. to C.*) Your Eminence was not always so . . . eminent.

10

CARDINAL. (*Remembering.*) Hy-e . . . (*Relishing each syllable.*) Hy-e-na. Hy. E. Na. We recall.

LAWYER. (*Steps in to* L. *chair. Close to break-through anger.*) We are close to Croesus, Your Eminence. I've brought gold with me . . . (*Leans forward.*) money, Your Eminence.

CARDINAL. (*Brushing it off.*) Yes, yes; later. Hy-e-na.

LAWYER. (*Sits* L. *chair. A threat, but quiet.*) A great deal of money, Your Eminence.

CARDINAL. We hear you, and we will discuss your business shortly. And why did we call you hyena . . . ?

LAWYER. (*Quiet threat again.*) If Croesus goes, he takes the gold away.

CARDINAL. (*Outgoing.*) But, Hyena, you are not Croesus; you are Croesus' emissary. You will wait; the gold will wait.

LAWYER. Are you certain?

CARDINAL. (*Ignoring the last.*) Ah, yes, it was in natural-science class, was it not? (*The Lawyer rises, moves away* L. *a little.*) Was it not?

LAWYER. (*Turns to Cardinal.*) Considering your mother's vagaries, you were never certain of your true father . . . were you?

CARDINAL. Correct, my child: considering one's mother's vagaries, one was never certain of one's true father . . . was one? But then, my child, we embraced the Church; and we *know* our true father. (*Pause, the Lawyer is silent. Crosses* L. *to birdcage.*) It was in natural-science class, eleven-five until noon, and did we not discover about the hyena . . .

LAWYER. (*Turns* R., *steps* R.) More money than you've ever seen!

CARDINAL. (*Parody, cool.*) Yum-yum. (*Back to former tone.*) Did we not discover about the hyena that it was a most resourceful scavenger? That, failing all other food, it would dine on offal . . .

LAWYER. (*Angrier.*) Millions!

CARDINAL. (*Pressing on.*) . . . and that it devoured the wounded and the dead? We found that last the most shocking: the dead. But we were young. And what horrified us most— (*Rises, crosses slowly* L. *to Lawyer.*) and, indeed, what gave us all the thought that the name was most fitting for yourself—

LAWYER. (*Ibid.*) Money!

CARDINAL. . . . was that to devour its dead, scavenged prey, it would often chew into it . . .

11

LAWYER. MONEY, YOU SWINE!

CARDINAL. (*Each word rising in pitch and volume.*) . . . chew into it THROUGH THE ANUS???? (*Both silent, breathing a little hard.*)

LAWYER. (*Finally, softly.*) Bastard.

CARDINAL. (*Quietly, too. Crosses* U. C., *puts fan on wall. Then sits* R. *chair.*) And now that we have brought the past to mind, and remembered what we could not exactly, shall we . . . talk business?

LAWYER. (*Softly, sadly.*) Robes the color of your mother's vice.

CARDINAL. (*Kindly.*) Come. Let us talk business. You are a businessman.

LAWYER. (*Sadly again.*) As are you.

CARDINAL. (*As if reminding a child of something.*) We are a Prince of the Church. Do you forget?

LAWYER. (*Suddenly turning* L. *and pointing to the cage, too off-hand.*) Are those two lovers? Do they mate?

CARDINAL. (*Patronizing, through the games.*) Come; let us talk business.

LAWYER. (*Persisting.*) Is it true? Do they? Even cardinals?

CARDINAL. (*A command.*) If you have money to give us . . . sit down and give it.

LAWYER. (*Turns to Cardinal.*) To the lay mind—to the cognoscenti it may be fact, accepted and put out of the head—but to the lay mind it's speculation . . . voyeuristic, perhaps, and certainly anti-Rome . . . mere speculation, but whispered about, even by the school children— *Crosses to* L. *of* L. *chair.*) indeed, as you must recall, the more . . . urbane of us wondered about the Fathers at school . . .

CARDINAL. . . . the more wicked . . .

LAWYER. . . . about their vaunted celibacy . . . among one another. Of course, we were at an age when everyone diddled everyone else . . .

CARDINAL. Some.

LAWYER. Yes, and I suppose it was natural enough for us to assume that the priests did too.

CARDINAL. (*As if changing the subject.*) You have . . . fallen away from the Church.

LAWYER. And into the arms of reason.

12

CARDINAL. (*Almost thinking of something else.*) An unsanctified union: not a marriage: a whore's bed.

LAWYER. A common-law marriage, for I am at law and, as you say, common. But it is quite respectable these days.

CARDINAL. (*Tough, bored with the church play-acting, heavy and tired.*) All right; that's enough. What's your business?

LAWYER. (*Pacing a little, after an appreciative smile. Crosses above L. chair, crushes out cigarette on wall, sits L. chair.*) My employer . . . wants to give some of her money to the Church.

CARDINAL. (*Enthusiastic, but guarded.*) Does she!

LAWYER. Gradually.

CARDINAL. (*Understanding.*) Ah-ha.

LAWYER. (*Offhand.*) A hundred million now.

CARDINAL. (*No shown surprise.*) And the rest gradually.

LAWYER. And the same amount each year for the next twenty— a hundred million a year. She is not ill; she has no intention of dying; she is quite young, youngish; there is no . . . rush.

CARDINAL. Indeed not.

LAWYER. It is that she is . . . overburdened with wealth.

CARDINAL. And it weighs on her soul.

LAWYER. Her soul is in excellent repair. If it were not, I doubt she'd be making the gesture. It is, as I said, that she is overburdened with wealth, and it . . . uh . . .

CARDINAL. (*Finding the words for him.*) . . . piles up.

LAWYER. (*A small smile.*) . . . and it is . . . wasted . . . lying about. It is one of several bequests—arrangements—she is making at the moment.

CARDINAL. (*Not astonishment, but unconcealed curiosity.*) One of several?

LAWYER. Yes. The Protestants as well, the Jews . . . hospitals, universities, orchestras, revolutions here and there . . .

CARDINAL. Well, we think it is a . . . responsible action. (*Rises, steps D.*) She is well, as you say.

LAWYER. Oh, yes; very.

CARDINAL. (*Crosses L. to L. of Lawyer.*) We are . . . glad. (*Turns R. to Lawyer. Amused fascination.*) How did you become her . . . lawyer, if we're not intruding upon . . . ?

LAWYER. (*Brief pause, light smile.*) She had a dossier on me, I suppose.

13

CARDINAL. It must be a great deal less revealing than ours . . . than our dossier on you.

LAWYER. Or a great deal *more* revealing.

CARDINAL. For her sake, and yours, we hope so.

LAWYER. To answer your question: I am a very good lawyer. It is as simple as that.

CARDINAL. (*Speculating on it.*) You *have* escaped prison.

LAWYER. I've done nothing to be imprisoned for.

CARDINAL. Pure. You're pure. You're ringed by stench, but you're pure. There's an odor that precedes you, and follows after you're gone, but you walk in the eye of it . . . pure.

LAWYER. (*Contemptuous.*) Look, pig, I don't enjoy you.

CARDINAL. (*Mockingly, his arms wide as if for an embrace.*) School chum!

LAWYER. If it were not my job to . . .

CARDINAL. (*Abruptly.*) Well, it is! Do it!

LAWYER. (*A smile to a hated but respected adversary.*) I've given you the facts: a hundred million a year for twenty years.

CARDINAL. But . . . ?

LAWYER. (*Shrugs.*) That's all.

CARDINAL. (*Stuttering with quiet excitement.*) Y-y-y-y-yes, b-b-but shall I just go to the *house* and pick it up in a *truck?*

LAWYER. (*Turns to Cardinal. Great, heavy relief.*) AAAAAAA-HHHHHHHHhhhhhhhhh.

CARDINAL. (*Caught up short.*) Hm? (*No reply.*) HM???

LAWYER. Say it again. Say it once again for me.

CARDINAL. (*Puzzled, suspicious.*) What? Say what?

LAWYER. (*Leaning over him.*) Say it again; repeat what you said. It was a sweet sound.

CARDINAL. (*Shouting.*) SAY WHAT!

LAWYER. (*Rises. Cooing into his ear.*) "Yes, but shall I just go to the house and pick it up in a truck?"

CARDINAL. (*Thinks on it a moment. Crosses* R. *to* D. *of* R. *chair.*) Well, perhaps there was a bit . . . perhaps there was too much levity there . . . uh, if one did not know one . . . (*Turns to Lawyer.*)

LAWYER. (*Coos again. Crosses slowly* R. *to Cardinal.*) . . . "But shall I just go to the house . . ."

CARDINAL. Wh . . . NO!

14

LAWYER. (*Sings it out. Backing Cardinal* R.) Shall IIIIIIII just go!

CARDINAL. (*Cross.*) No! We . . . we did not say that!

LAWYER. IIIIIIIIIIIIII.

CARDINAL. (*A threat.*) We did not say "I."

LAWYER. (*Almost baby talk.*) We said I. Yes, we did; we said I. (*Cardinal* D. R. *of fountain. Lawyer* L. *of fountain. Suddenly loud and tough.*) We said I, and we said it straight. I! I! I! By God, we picked up our skirts and lunged for it! IIIIIII! Me! Me! Gimme!

CARDINAL. (*Full shout.*) WE SAID NO SUCH THING!

LAWYER. (*Crosses* L., *sits* R. *chair. Oily imitation.*) We reserve the first-person singular, do we not, for . . . for intimates, equals . . . or superiors. (*Harsher.*) Well, my dear, you found all three applying. Intimate. How close would we rub to someone for all that wealth? As close as we once did?

CARDINAL. (*Not wanting to hear, but weak.*) Leave . . . leave off.

LAWYER. (*Pressing.*) Equals? Oh, money equals anything you want. Levels! LEVELS THE EARTH! AND THE HEAVENS!

CARDINAL. (*Step* L.) ENOUGH!!

LAWYER. (*The final thrust.*) . . . Or superiors. Who is superior, the one who stands on the mount of heaven? (*Rises, crosses* R. *to Cardinal.*) We think not! We have come down off our plural . . . when the stakes are high enough . . . and the hand, the kissed hand palsies out . . . FOR THE LOOT!!

CARDINAL. (*Hissed.*) Satan!

LAWYER. (*After a pause.*) Satan? You would believe it . . . if you believed in God. (*Breaks into—for lack of a better word— Satanic laughter, subsides. Cardinal turns* U., *uses handkerchief. Lawyer crosses* L. *to* C. *Patronizing now.*) No, poor Eminence, you don't have to drive a truck around to the back door for it. We'll get the money to you . . . to your . . . people. Fact, I don't want you coming 'round . . . at all. Clacketing through the great corridors of the place, sizing it up, not content with enough wealth to buy off the first two hundred saints picked out of a bag, but wondering if *it* mightn't get thrown into the bargain as a . . . summer residence, perhaps . . . uh, after she dies and scoots up to heaven. (*Lawyer picks up walking stick.*)

CARDINAL. (*On his feet, but shaky, uncertain.*) This . . . uh . . .

LAWYER. . . . interview is terminated?

CARDINAL. (*Quietly.*) This is unseemly talk.

LAWYER. (*Vastly, wryly amused.*) Oh? Is it?

CARDINAL. (*Turns* R. *A mechanical toy breaking down.*) We will . . . we will forgive your presumption, your . . . excess . . . excuse, yes . . . excuse? . . . We will . . . overlook your . . . (*Crosses* R., *sits* R. *chair. A plea is underneath.*) Let us have no more of this talk. It *is* unseemly.

LAWYER. (*At* C. *Businesslike, as if the preceding speech had not happened.*) As I said, I don't want you coming 'round . . . bothering her.

CARDINAL. (*Humble.*) I would not bother the lady; I have not met her. Of course, I would very much like to have the pleasure of . . .

LAWYER. We slip often now, don't we.

CARDINAL. (*Very soul-weary.*) Pardon?

LAWYER. The plural is gone out of us, I see.

CARDINAL. Ah. Well. Perhaps.

LAWYER. Regird yourself. We *are* about terminated. (*Quick, insulting finger-snaps.*) Come! Come! Back up; back on your majesty! Hup!

CARDINAL. (*Slowly, wearily coming back into shape.*) Uh . . . yes . . . of—of course. We, uh, we shall make any arrangements you wish (*Rises slowly.*) . . . naturally. We . . . we have no desire to intrude ourselves upon . . . uh . . . upon . . .

LAWYER. Miss Alice.

CARDINAL. Yes; upon Miss Alice. If she . . . if Miss Alice desires privacy, certainly her generosity has earned it for her. We . . . would not intrude.

LAWYER. You *are* kind. (*Fishing in a pocket for a notebook.*) What . . . is . . . your . . . secretary's . . . name . . . I think I have it . . . right . . . (*Finds notebook.*)

CARDINAL. Brother . . .

LAWYER. Julian! Is that not right?

CARDINAL. Yes, Brother Julian. He is an old friend of ours; we . . .

LAWYER. Rather daring of you, wasn't it? Choosing a lay brother as your private secretary?

CARDINAL. (*A combination of apology and defiance.*) He is an old friend of ours, and he has served the . . .

LAWYER. (*Praising a puppy.*) You are adventurous, are you not?

16

CARDINAL. He has been assigned many years to the . . .

LAWYER. (*Waving his notebook a little.*) We have it; all down; we know. (*Puts notebook away.*)

CARDINAL. (*A little sadly.*) Ah-ha.

LAWYER. Yes. Well, we will send for your . . . Brother Julian. . . . To clear up odds and ends. Every bank has its runners. We don't ask vice presidents to . . . fetch and carry. Inform Your Brother Julian. We will send for him. (*Lawyer turns L. and exits L.*)

CARDINAL. (*Crosses U. into alcove. To the exiting figure.*) Yes, we . . . will. (*Stands still, looks at the ground, tired, looks at his sleeves, his fingernails, his ring, up, out, over. Sighs, looks at the cage. Smiles slightly, moves to the cage, the fingers of his left hand fluttering at it.*) Do . . . do you . . . do you have much to say to one another, my dears? Do you? You find it comforting? Hmmmmmmm? Do you? Hmmmm? Do-do-do-do-do-do-do? Hmmmmmm? Do?

CURTAIN

ACT I

SCENE 2

The library of a mansion—a castle. Pillared walls, floor-to-ceiling leather-bound books. A great arched doorway, U. C. A huge reading table to L.—practical. A phreno-logical head on it. To R., jutting out of the wings, a huge doll's-house model of the building of which the present room is a part. It is as tall as a man, and a good deal of it must be visible from all parts of the audience. An alternative—and perhaps more practical—would be for the arched doorway to be either L. or R., with bookshelves to both sides of the set, coming toward C., and to have the entire doll's house in the rear wall, in which case it could be smaller—say, twelve feet long and proportion-ately high. At any rate, it is essential. At rise, Julian, carrying briefcase, crosses in arch from R., stops, then crosses D. L., steps to D. L.

JULIAN. Extraordinary . . . (*Crosses* U. *to* R. C. *of model. After a few moments of head-shaking concentration.*) extraordinary.
BUTLER. (*Crosses in from* L. *with chamois and three spoons. After entering, observing Julian, not having heard him. He leans on banister.*) Extraordinary, isn't it?
JULIAN. (*Mildly startled.*) Uh . . . yes, unbelievable . . . (*Agreeing.*) Extraordinary.
BUTLER. (*Crosses to top of* L. *steps. He moves about with a kind of unbutlerlike ease.*) I never cease to wonder at the . . . the fact of it, I suppose.
JULIAN. The workmanship . . .
BUTLER. (*A mild correction.*) That someone would do it.
JULIAN. (*Seeing.*) Yes, yes.
BUTLER. (*Crosses down* L. *steps to* U. L. C.) That someone would . . . well, for heaven's sake, that someone would build . . . (*Refers to the set.*) . . . this . . . castle? . . . and then . . . duplicate it in such precise miniature, so exactly. Have you looked through the windows?
JULIAN. No, I . . .
BUTLER. It is exact. Look and see.
JULIAN. (*Moves even closer to the model, peers through a tiny window at* R. C.) Why . . . why, YES. I . . . there's a great . . . baronial dining room, even with tiny candlesticks on the tables!
BUTLER. (*Nodding his head, a thumb back over his shoulder.*) It's down the hall, off the hallway to the right.
JULIAN. (*The proper words won't come.*) It's . . . it's . . .
BUTLER. (*Sits* L. C. *ledge of model.*) Look over here. There; right there.
JULIAN. (*Peers at model,* L. *of* C.) It's . . . it's this room! This room we're in!
BUTLER. Yes.
JULIAN. Extraordinary.
BUTLER. Is there anyone there? Are we there?
JULIAN. (*Briefly startled, then laughs, looks back into the model.*) Uh . . . no. It seems to be quite . . . empty.
BUTLER. (*A quiet smile.*) One feels one should see one's self . . . almost.
JULIAN. (*Looks back to him, after a brief, thoughtful pause.*) Yes. That would be rather a shock, wouldn't it?

18

BUTLER. Did you notice . . . did you notice that there is a model within that room in the castle? A model of the model?

JULIAN. I . . . I did. But . . . I didn't register it, it seemed so . . . continual.

BUTLER. (*A shy smile.*) You don't suppose that within that tiny model in the model there, there is . . . another room like this, with yet a tinier model within it, and within . . .

JULIAN. (*Laughs.*) . . . and within and within and within and . . . ? No, I . . . rather doubt it. It's remarkable craftsmanship, though. Remarkable.

BUTLER. (*Crosses to sideboard, puts spoons in* U. *drawer, shuts drawer.*) Hell to clean.

JULIAN. (*Crosses to* R. *end of model, looks at roof. Conversational enthusiasm.*) Yes! I should think so! Does it open from . . .

BUTLER. It's sealed. Tight. There is no dust.

JULIAN. (*Disappointed at being joked with.*) Oh.

BUTLER. (*Dusts salver on sideboard.*) I was sporting.

JULIAN. (*Crosses* D. L. *to* L. *chair.*) Oh.

BUTLER. (*Puts down salver. Crosses* D. *of* L. *chair. Straight curiosity.*) Did you mind?

JULIAN. (*Too free.*) I? No!

BUTLER. (*Doctrine, no sarcasm.*) It would almost be taken for granted (*Julian starts to sit* L. *chair. Butler moves and blocks seat. Julian crosses* R. *to* R. C.) one would think—that if a person or a person's surrogate went to the trouble, and expense, of having such a dream toy made, that the person would have it sealed, so that there'd be no dust. (*Julian puts briefcase on cigarette box,* C. *of* R. *table.*) Wouldn't one think.

JULIAN. (*Sarcasm and embarrassment together.*) One would think. (*He sits* R. C. *chair.*)

BUTLER. (*Crosses* R. *to* U. *of table. Gives briefcase to Julian. After a pause, some rue.*) I have enough to do as it is.

JULIAN. (*Eager to move on to something else.*) Yes, yes!

BUTLER. (*Picks up cigarette box and dusts.*) It's enormous . . . (*A sudden thought.*) even for a castle, I suppose. (*Points to the model. Julian looks at model.*) Not that. (*Now to the room.*) This.

JULIAN. Endless! You . . . certainly you don't work alone.

BUTLER. Oh, Christ, no. (*Puts down cigarette box.*)

JULIAN. (*Reaffirming.*) I would have thought.

19

BUTLER. (*Almost daring him to disagree.*) Still, there's enough work.

JULIAN. (*Slightly testy.*) I'm sure. (*A pause between them.*)

BUTLER. (*Flicks dustcloth at mantel, then turns* D. *For no reason, a sort of "Oh, what the hell."*) Heigh-ho.

JULIAN. Will there be . . . someone? . . . to see me? . . . soon?

BUTLER. Hm?

JULIAN. (*Rises, steps* D.) Will there be someone to see me soon! (*After a blank stare from the other.*) You announced me? I trust?

BUTLER. (*Snapping to.*) Oh! Yes! (*Laughs.*) Sorry. Uh . . . yes, there will be someone to see you soon.

JULIAN. (*Attempt at good-fellowship.*) Ah, good! (*Julian crosses* L. *to sideboard, looks at phrenological head.*)

BUTLER. Are you a priest? (*Crosses to* C.)

JULIAN. (*Self-demeaning.*) I? No, no . . .

BUTLER. If not Catholic, Episcopal.

JULIAN. No . . .

BUTLER. What, then?

JULIAN. (*Turns to Butler. Steps* L. *of* L. *chair.*) I am a lay brother. I am not ordained.

BUTLER. You are *of* the cloth but have not taken it.

JULIAN. (*None too happy.*) You *could* say that.

BUTLER. (*No trifling.*) One *could* say it, and quite accurately. (*Julian sits* L. *chair.*) May I get you some ice water? (*Butler shakes head "no." Julian rises, crosses* R. *to* R. C.)

JULIAN. (*Put off and confused.*) No!

BUTLER. (*Feigns apology.*) Sorry.

JULIAN. You must forgive me. (*Almost childlike enthusiasm.*) This is rather a big day for me.

BUTLER. (*Nods understandingly.*) Iced tea.

JULIAN. (*Turns to Butler. Laughs.*) No . . . nothing, thank you . . . uh . . . I don't have your name.

BUTLER. Fortunate.

JULIAN. No, I meant that . . .

BUTLER. Butler.

JULIAN. Pardon?

BUTLER. Butler.

JULIAN. Yes. You . . . you *are* the butler, are you not, but . . .

BUTLER. Butler. My name is Butler.

JULIAN. (*Innocent pleasure.*) How extraordinary!

BUTLER. (*Putting it aside.*) No, not really. Appropriate: Butler . . . butler. If my name were Carpenter, and I were a butler . . . or if I *were* a carpenter, and my name were Butler . . .

JULIAN. But *still* . . .

BUTLER. . . . it would not be so appropriate. And think: if I were a woman, and had become a chambermaid, say, and my name were Butler . . .

JULIAN. (*Anticipating.*) . . . you would be in for some rather tiresome exchanges.

BUTLER. (*Steps L. Cutting, but light.*) None more than this.

JULIAN. (*Sadly.*) Aha.

BUTLER. (*Forgiving.*) Coffee, then.

JULIAN. (*As if he can't explain.*) No. Nothing. (*Lawyer enters from U. L.*)

BUTLER. (*Semi-serious bow.*) I am at your service.

LAWYER. I, too. (*Butler crosses to sideboard, takes off apron.*)

JULIAN. Ah!

LAWYER. I'm sorry to have kept you waiting, but . . . (*Crosses down L. steps to R. of L. chair.*)

JULIAN. Oh, no, no . . .

LAWYER. . . . I was conferring with Miss Alice.

JULIAN. Yes.

LAWYER. (*To Butler, no fondness.*) Dearest.

BUTLER. (*To Lawyer, same.*) Darling.

LAWYER. (*To Julian.*) Doubtless, though, you two have . . . (*Waves a hand about.*)

JULIAN. Oh, we've had a most . . . unusual . . .

LAWYER. (*To Butler, ignoring Julian's answer.*) You've offered our guest refreshments?

JULIAN. (*Offering hand.*) Brother Julian.

BUTLER. (*Turns to C., steps D.*) Ice water, iced tea, and coffee —hot assumed, I imagine—none taken.

LAWYER. Gracious! (*Back to Julian.*) Port, perhaps. Removed people take port, I've noticed.

JULIAN. (*More to please than anything.*) Yes. Port. Please.

LAWYER. (*To Butler.*) Port for . . .

JULIAN. (*Crosses to R. C. chair, picks up briefcase, sits.*) Julian —Brother Julian. (*Butler crosses to sideboard, puts apron away. Takes out port and glass, pours port, puts glass on salver.*)

21

LAWYER. (*Slightly patronizing.*) I know. (*Crosses* R. *to* R. *of table.*) I would join you, but it is not my habit to drink before sundown. Not a condemnation, you understand. One of my minor disciplines.

BUTLER. (*Generally, looking at the decanter.*) The port is eighteen-oh-six. (*To the Lawyer.*) How do they fortify wines, again?

JULIAN. Alcohol is added, more alcohol . . . at the time of casking. Fortify . . . strengthen.

BUTLER. Ah, yes.

LAWYER. (*To Julian.*) Of course, your grandfather was a vintner, was he not.

JULIAN. Goodness, you . . . you have my history.

LAWYER. Oh, we do. (*Crosses* U. *of table.*) Such a mild life . . . save those six years in your thirties which are . . . blank . . . in our report on you. (*Butler crossing* R. *with port to* L. *of Julian.*)

JULIAN. (*A good covering laugh.*) Oh, they were . . . mild, in their own way. Blank, but not black.

LAWYER. (*Sits* C. *chair.*) Will you fill them for us? The blank years?

JULIAN. (*Taking the glass from Butler.*) Thank you. (*The laugh again.*) They were nothing.

LAWYER. (*Steelier.*) Still, you will fill them for us.

JULIAN. (*Pleasant, but very firm.*) No.

BUTLER. Gracious!

LAWYER. Recalcitrance, yes . . . well, we must have our people dig further.

JULIAN. You'll find nothing interesting. You'll find some . . . upheaval, but . . . waste, mostly. Dull waste.

LAWYER. The look of most of our vices in retrospect, eh?

BUTLER. (*Crosses* D. L. *Light.*) I have fleshpot visions: carousals, thighs and heavy perfume. . . .

LAWYER. (*Rises, crosses* U. C. *To Butler.*) It's in your mind, fitting, a mind worthy of your name. (*To Julian.*) Did you two . . . did he tell you his name, and did you two have a veritable badminton over it? Puns and chuckles?

JULIAN. We . . . labored it a bit, I more than . . . Butler, it would appear.

BUTLER. I was churlish, I'm sorry. If there weren't so many of you and only one of *me* . . .

JULIAN. Oh, now . . . (*Butler crosses to sideboard.*)

LAWYER. (*Still on it.*) You're not going to tell me about those six years, eh?

JULIAN. (*Stares at him for a moment, then says it clearly, enunciating.*) No. (*Lawyer shrugs.*)

BUTLER. (*Gets glass, pours port.*) May I have some port?

LAWYER. (*Slightly incredulous.*) Do you like port?

BUTLER. (*Crosses R. to D. R. chair, with glass.*) Not very, but I thought I'd keep him company while you play police.

LAWYER. (*Shrugs again.*) It's not my house. (*Turns to Julian.*) One can't say, "It's not my castle," can one? (*Back to Butler.*) If you think it's proper.

BUTLER. Well, with the wine cellar stacked like a munitions dump, and you "never having any" until the barn swallows start screeping around . . .

LAWYER. There's no such word as screep.

BUTLER. (*Shrugs. Sits D. R. chair.*) Fit.

JULIAN. I think it has a nice onomatopoetic ring about it . . .

LAWYER. (*Down to business, rather rudely.*) Your buddy told you why we sent for you?

JULIAN. (*Offended, but pretending confusion.*) My . . . buddy?

LAWYER. Mine, really. We were at school together. Did he tell you that? (*As Julian intentionally looks blank.*) His Eminence.

JULIAN. Ah!

LAWYER. (*Imitation.*) Ah! (*Snapped.*) Well? Did he?

JULIAN. (*Choosing his words carefully, precisely.*) His Eminence informed me . . . generally. He called me into his . . .

LAWYER. . . . garden . . .

JULIAN. . . . garden . . . which is a comfortable office in summer . . .

BUTLER. Ninety-six today.

JULIAN. (*Interested.*) Indeed!

BUTLER. More tomorrow.

LAWYER. (*Impatiently.*) Called you into his garden.

JULIAN. And—sorry—and . . . told me of the high honor which he had chosen for me.

LAWYER. (*Scoffing.*) He. Chosen. You.

JULIAN. Of . . . your lady's most . . .

23

LAWYER. Miss Alice.

JULIAN. Of Miss Alice's— (*Rises, steps to Lawyer.*) sorry, I've not met the lady yet, and first names—of her overwhelming bequest to the Church . . .

LAWYER. Not a bequest; a bequest is made in a will; Miss Alice is not dead.

JULIAN. Uh . . . grant?

LAWYER. Grant.

JULIAN. (*Taking a deep breath.*) Of her overwhelming grant to the Church, and of my assignment to come here, to take care of . . .

LAWYER. Odds and ends.

JULIAN. (*Shrugs one shoulder.*) . . . if you like. "A few questions and answers" was how it was put to me.

BUTLER. (*Rises, steps D. and L. To Lawyer, impressed.*) He's a lay brother.

LAWYER. (*Bored.*) We know. (*For Julian's benefit.*) His Eminence—buddy . . . (*Julian turns R., crosses R. to L. of table. Gives glass to Butler.*)

JULIAN. (*Natural, sincere.*) Tch-tch-tch-tch-tch . . .

LAWYER. He was my buddy at school . . . if you don't mind. (*Beginning, now, to Butler, but quickly becoming general. Butler crosses L. with glasses.*) His Eminence—though you have never met him, Butler, seen him, perhaps—is a most (*Butler stops D. L. of L. chair. Lawyer moves R. of L. chair.*) . . . eminent man; and bold, very bold; behind—or, underneath—what would seem to be a solid rock of . . . pomposity, sham, peacocking, there is a . . . flows a secret river . . . of . . .

BUTLER. (*Crosses to sideboard. Puts down Julian's glass. For Julian's benefit.*) This is an endless metaphor.

LAWYER. . . . of unconventionality, defiance, even. Simple sentences? Is that all you·want? Did you know that Brother Julian here is the only lay brother in the history of Christendom assigned, chosen, as secretary and confidant to a Prince of the Church? Ever?

JULIAN. (*Mildly.*) That is not known as fact.

LAWYER. Name others!

JULIAN. (*Crosses L. to C.*) I say it is not known as fact. I grant it is not usual—my appointment as secretary to His Eminence. . . .

LAWYER. (*Faint disgust.*) An honor, at any rate, an unusual

24

honor for a lay brother, an honor accorded by a most unusual Prince of the Church—a prince of a man, in fact—a prince whose still waters . . . well, you finish it.

BUTLER. (*Pretending puzzlement as to how to finish it.*) . . . whose still waters . . .

JULIAN. His Eminence is, indeed, a most unusual man.

LAWYER. (*Sourly.*) I said he was a prince.

BUTLER. (*Pretending to be talking to himself.*) . . . run quiet? Run deep? Run *deep! That's* good!

LAWYER. Weren't there a few eyebrows raised at your appointment?

JULIAN. There . . . I was not informed of it . . . if there were. His Eminence would not burden me. . . .

LAWYER. (*Still to Julian, patronizing.*) He is really Santa Claus; we know.

JULIAN. (*Rising to it.*) Your animosity toward His Eminence must make your task very difficult for you. I must say I . . .

LAWYER. I have learned . . . (*Brief pause before he says the name with some distaste.*) Brother Julian . . . never to confuse the representative of a . . . thing with the thing itself.

BUTLER. (*Steps R. to Lawyer.*) . . . though I wonder if you'd intended to get involved in *two* watery metaphors there: underground river, and still waters.

LAWYER. (*To Butler.*) No, I had not. (*Butler turns, crosses to U. of sideboard. Back to Julian.*) A thing with its representative. Your Cardinal and I loathe one another, and I find him unworthy of contempt. (*A hand up to stop any coming objection.*) A cynic and a hypocrite, a posturer, but all the same the representative of an august and revered . . . body.

JULIAN. (*Murmured.*) You are most unjust.

LAWYER. (*As if he were continuing a prepared speech.*) Uh . . . revered body. And Rome, in its perhaps wily—though certainly inscrutable—wisdom, Rome has found reason to appoint that wreckage as its representative.

JULIAN. Really, I can't permit you to talk that way.

LAWYER. You will permit it, you're under instructions, you have a job to do. In fact, you have this present job because I cannot stand your Cardinal.

JULIAN. He . . . he did not tell me so.

25

LAWYER. *We* tell you so. (*Julian dips his head to one side in a "perhaps it is true" gesture.*) And it is so.

JULIAN. (*Turns* R., *crosses to* R. C.) I will not . . . I will not concern myself with . . . all this.

BUTLER. (*Butler crosses* D. *to* L. *of* L. *chair. Quite to himself.*) I don't like port.

LAWYER. (*To Butler.*) Then don't drink it. (*To Julian. Steps* R.) You're quite right: bow your head, stop up your ears and do what you're told.

JULIAN. Obedience is not a fault.

LAWYER. Nor always a virtue. See Fascism.

JULIAN. (*Picks up briefcase, steps* L. *Rather strong for him.*) Perhaps we can get on with our business. . . .

LAWYER. (*He, too.*) You don't want to take up my time, or your own.

JULIAN. Yes.

BUTLER. (*Crosses to sideboard. Puts down glass.*) Then I won't drink it.

LAWYER. (*To Julian, briskly, as to a servant.*) All right! I shall tell Miss Alice you've come—that the drab fledgling is pecking away in the library, impatient for . . . food for the Church.

JULIAN. (*A tight smile, a tiny formal bow.*) If you would be so kind.

LAWYER. (*Twisting the knife.*) I'll find out if she cares to see you today. (*Starts out* L. *steps.*)

JULIAN. (*Ibid.*) Please.

LAWYER. (*Moving toward the archway.*) And, if she cares to, I will have you brought up.

JULIAN. (*Steps* U. *Mild surprise, but not a question.*) Up.

LAWYER. (*At* C. *platform. Almost challenging him.*) Up. (*Pause.*) You will not tell us about the six years—those years blank but not black . . . the waste, the dull waste. (*Butler crosses to top of first level,* L.)

JULIAN. (*Small smile.*) No.

LAWYER. (*He, too.*) You will . . . in time. (*To Butler.*) Won't he, Butler? Time? The great revealer? (*Lawyer exits, closes doors. Butler sits on banister.*)

JULIAN. (*After the Lawyer is gone, no indignation.*) Well.

BUTLER. (*Offhand.*) Nasty man.

26

JULIAN. (*Intentionally feigning surprise.*) Oh? (*He and Butler laugh.*) Up. (*Crosses to* C.)
BUTLER. Sir?
JULIAN. Up.
BUTLER. Oh! Yes! She . . . (*Moves to the model.*) has her apartments up . . . here. (*He points to a tower area.*) Here.
JULIAN. (*Crosses to* L. *tower, looks.*) A-ha.
BUTLER. (*Crosses down* L. *steps to* U. *of* L. *chair. Straightening things up.*) About those six years . . .
JULIAN. (*Not unfriendly, very matter-of-fact. Crosses* D. *to* C.) What of them?
BUTLER. Yes, what of them?
JULIAN. Oh . . . (*Pause.*) I . . . I lost my faith. (*Pause.*) In God.
BUTLER. Ah. (*Then a questioning look.*)
JULIAN. Is there more?
BUTLER. *Is* there more?
JULIAN. Well, nothing . . . of matter. I . . . declined. I . . . shriveled into myself; a glass dome . . . descended, and it seemed I was out of reach, unreachable, finally unreaching, in this . . . paralysis, of sorts. I . . . put myself in a mental home.
BUTLER. (*Butler crosses* D. L. *of* L. *chair. Curiously noncommittal.*) Ah.
JULIAN. (*Crosses to Butler.*) I could not reconcile myself to the chasm between the nature of God and the use to which men put . . . God.
BUTLER. Between your God and others', your view and theirs.
JULIAN. I said what I intended: (*Weighs the opposites in each hand.*) It is God the mover, not God the puppet; God the creator, not the God created by man.
BUTLER. (*Almost pitying.*) Six years in the loony bin for semantics?
JULIAN. (*Slightly flustered, beat.*) It is not semantics! Men create a false God in their own image, it is easier for them! . . . It is not . . .
BUTLER. Levity! Forget it!
JULIAN. I . . . yes. (*A chime sounds.*)
BUTLER. (*Crosses up* L. *steps, picks up coat on post, puts it on. Julian crosses to* R. C. *chair, picks up briefcase, crosses to* L. *steps and up to top.*) Miss Alice will see you. I will take you up.

JULIAN. (*Butler at doors, Julian on top step.*) Forgive me . . .
I . . .
BUTLER. (*Butler opens R. door. Moves toward archway.*) Let me
show you up.
JULIAN. (*Steps to C.*) You *did* ask me.
BUTLER. (*Level.*) Yes, and you told me.
JULIAN. (*An explanation, not an apology.*) My faith and my
sanity . . . they are one and the same.
BUTLER. Yes? (*Considers it.*) A-ha. (*Smiles noncommittally.*)
We must not keep the lady waiting. (*They begin exiting L.,
Butler preceding Julian.*)

CURTAIN

ACT I

SCENE 3

*An upstairs sitting room of the castle. Feminine, but not
frilly. Blues instead of pinks. Fireplace in keeping with the
castle. A door to the bedroom in the rear wall, R.; a door
from the hallway in the side wall, R.*
AT RISE: *Miss Alice is seated in a wing chair, facing windows, its back to the audience, the Lawyer is at L. of her
chair, facing her.*

LAWYER. (*Pause, he has finished one sentence, is pondering another.*) . . . Nor is it as simple as all that. The instinct of giving
may die out in our time—if you'll grant that giving is an instinct.
The government is far more interested in taking, in regulated taking, than in promoting spontaneous generosity. Remember what I
told you—what we discussed—in reference to the charitable
foundations, and how . . . (*A knock on the hall door. Lawyer
crosses to C.*) That will be our bird of prey. Pray. P-R-A-Y. What
a pun I could make on that; bird of pray. Come in. (*The hall
doors open, Butler precedes Julian into the room.*)
BUTLER. (*Steps U. of door, turns D.*) Brother Julian, who *was* in
the library, is now here.
LAWYER. So he is. (*To Julian, impatiently.*) Come in, come in.

28

JULIAN. (*Crosses to Lawyer. Carries briefcase.*) Yes . . . certainly.

BUTLER. (*Crosses to doors, R.*) May I go? I'm tired.

LAWYER. (*Grandly.*) By all means.

BUTLER. (*Turns to go.*) Thank you. (*To Julian.*) Goodbye.

JULIAN. Goodb . . . I'll . . . we'll see one another again?

BUTLER. Oh. Yes, probably. (*As he exits.*) Goodbye, everybody. (*Shuts doors. Julian steps D. R.*)

LAWYER. (*After Butler exits, chuckles.*) What is it the nouveaux riches are always saying? "You can't get good servants nowadays"?

JULIAN. He seems . . .

LAWYER. (*Curt.*) He is very good. (*At R. of chair. Turns to the chair.*) Miss Alice, our Brother Julian is here. (*Repeats it, louder.*) OUR BROTHER JULIAN IS HERE. (*To Julian.*) She's terribly hard of hearing. (*To Miss Alice.*) DO YOU WANT TO SEE HIM? (*To Julian.*) I think she's responding. Sometimes . . . well, at her age and condition . . . twenty minutes can go by . . . for her to assimilate a sentence and reply to it.

JULIAN. But I thought . . . His Eminence said she was . . . young.

LAWYER. (*Crosses above to L. of chair.*) SHHHHHHHH! She's moving. (*Miss Alice slowly rises from her chair and comes around it to D. of chair. Her face is that of a withered crone, her hair gray and white and matted, she is bent, she moves with two canes.*)

MISS ALICE. (*Finally, with a cracked and ancient voice, to Julian.*) Hello there, young man.

LAWYER. (*As Julian takes a step forward.*) Hah! Don't come too close, you'll unnerve her.

JULIAN. But I'm terribly puzzled. I was led to believe that she was a young woman, and . . .

MISS ALICE. Hello there, young man.

LAWYER. Speak to her.

JULIAN. Miss . . . Miss Alice, how do you do?

LAWYER. Louder.

JULIAN. HOW DO YOU DO?

MISS ALICE. (*To Lawyer.*) How do I do *what*?

LAWYER. It's a formality.

MISS ALICE. WHAT!?

LAWYER. IT IS A FORMALITY, AN OPENING GAMBIT.

29

MISS ALICE. Oh. (*To Julian.*) How do you do?

JULIAN. Very well . . . thank you.

MISS ALICE. WHAT!?

JULIAN. VERY WELL, THANK YOU.

MISS ALICE. Don't you scream at me!

JULIAN. (*Mumbled.*) Sorry.

MISS ALICE. WHAT!?

JULIAN. SORRY!

MISS ALICE. (*Almost a pout.*) Oh.

LAWYER. (*Who has enjoyed this, crosses above to R. doors.*) Well, I think I'll leave you two now . . . for your business. I'm sure you'll have a . . .

JULIAN. (*An attempted urgent aside to the Lawyer. Crosses u. to Lawyer. Miss Alice counters L.*) Do you think you . . . shouldn't you be here? You've . . . you've had more experience with her, and . . .

LAWYER. (*Laughing.*) No, no, you'll get along fine. (*Crosses D. L. To Miss Alice.*) I'LL LEAVE YOU TWO TOGETHER NOW. (*Miss Alice nods vigorously.*) HIS NAME IS BROTHER JULIAN, AND THERE ARE SIX YEARS MISSING FROM HIS LIFE. (*She nods again.*) I'LL BE DOWNSTAIRS. (*Crosses R. to door. Begins to leave.*)

MISS ALICE. (*When the Lawyer is at the door.*) Don't steal anything.

LAWYER. (*Exiting.*) ALL RIGHT! (*Shuts doors.*)

JULIAN. (*After a pause, begins bravely, taking a step forward. Crosses L. to Miss Alice.*) Perhaps you should sit down. Let me . . .

MISS ALICE. WHAT!?

JULIAN. PERHAPS YOU SHOULD SIT DOWN!

MISS ALICE. (*Not fear, malevolence.*) Keep away from me!

JULIAN. Sorry. (*To himself. Crosses D. of Miss Alice to L. of her.*) Oh, really, this is impossible.

MISS ALICE. WHAT!?

JULIAN. I SAID THIS WAS IMPOSSIBLE.

MISS ALICE. (*Thinks about that for a moment, then.*) If you're a defrocked priest, what're you doing in all that? (*Pointing to Julian's garb.*)

JULIAN. I AM NOT A DEFROCKED PRIEST, I AM A LAY BROTHER. I HAVE NEVER BEEN A PRIEST.

MISS ALICE. What did you drink downstairs?

JULIAN. I had a glass of port . . . PORT!

MISS ALICE. (*A spoiled, crafty child.*) You didn't bring *me* one.

JULIAN. I had no idea you . . .

MISS ALICE. WHAT!?

JULIAN. (*Crosses* R. *to* C.) SHALL I GET YOU A GLASS?

MISS ALICE. A glass of *what*.

JULIAN. PORT. A GLASS OF PORT.

MISS ALICE. (*As if be were crazy.*) What for?

JULIAN. BECAUSE YOU . . . (*Crosses* R. *to doors. To himself again.*) Really, this won't do.

MISS ALICE. (*Straightening up, ridding herself of the canes, assuming a normal voice. Crosses to* U. L., *drops lap rug on ottoman.*) I agree with you, it won't do, really.

JULIAN. (*Astonishment.*) I beg your pardon?

MISS ALICE. I said it won't do at all. (*She unfastens and removes her wig, unties and takes off her mask, becomes herself, as Julian watches. openmouthed.*) There. Is that better? And you needn't yell at me any more; if anything, my hearing is *too* good. (*Crosses* L. *to mirror.*)

JULIAN. (*Slightly put out.*) I . . . I don't understand.

MISS ALICE. Are you annoyed?

JULIAN. I suspect I will be . . . might be . . . after the surprise leaves me.

MISS ALICE. (*Smiling.*) Don't be; it's only a little game.

JULIAN. Yes, doubtless. But why?

MISS ALICE. (*Crosses to* C., *extends band.*) Oh, indulge us, please.

JULIAN. (*Taking her hand.*) Well, of course, it would be my pleasure . . . but, considering the importance of our meeting . . .

MISS ALICE. Exactly. Considering the importance of our meeting.

JULIAN. A . . . a test for me.

MISS ALICE. (*Laughs.*) No, not at all, a little lightness to counter the weight. (*Mock seriousness.*) For we are involved in weighty matters . . . the transfer of millions, the rocking of empires. (*Normal, light tone again.*) Let's be comfortable, shall we? (*Miss Alice crosses* L. *to ottoman. Folds lap rug, throws it on floor.*) Swing my chair around. (*Julian moves to do so.*) As you can see —you can, I trust—I'm *not* a hundred and thirteen years old, but

31

I *do* have my crotchets, even now: I have chairs everywhere that are mine—in each room . . . a chair that is mine, that I alone use.

JULIAN. (*Moving the chair.*) Where would you . . . (*Swings chair to face* D.)

MISS ALICE. (*Lightly.*) Just . . . swing it . . . around. You needn't move it. Good. (*Miss Alice crosses* D., *sits in chair.*) Now, sit with me. (*Julian crosses* U. *of chair, sits on ottoman.*) Fine. In the dining room, of course, there is no question—I sit at the head of the table. But, in the drawing rooms, or the library, or whatever room you wish to mention, I have a chair that I consider my possession.

JULIAN. But you possess the entire . . . (*Thinks of a word.*) establishment.

MISS ALICE. Of course, but it is such a large . . . establishment that one needs the feel of specific possession in every . . . area.

JULIAN. (*Rather shy, but pleasant.*) Do you become . . . cross if someone accidentally assumes your chair, one of your chairs?

MISS ALICE. (*Thinks about it, then.*) How odd! Curiously, it has never happened, so I cannot say. Tell me about yourself.

JULIAN. Well, there isn't much to say . . . much that isn't already known. Your lawyer would seem to have assembled a case book on me, and . . .

MISS ALICE. Yes, yes, but not the things that would interest him, the things that would interest me.

JULIAN. (*Genuine interest.*) And what are they?

MISS ALICE. (*Laughs again.*) Let me see. (*Julian rises, steps* L. *Leaves briefcase on ottoman.*) Ah! Do I terrify you?

JULIAN. (*Wipes hands.*) You *did*, and you are still . . . awesome.

MISS ALICE. (*Sweetly.*) Thank you. Did my lawyer intimidate you?

JULIAN. It would seem to be his nature—or his pleasure—to intimidate, and . . . well, I am, perhaps, more easily intimidated than some.

MISS ALICE. Perhaps you are, but he *is* a professional. And how did you find Butler?

JULIAN. A gentle man, quick . . . but mostly gentle.

MISS ALICE. Gentle, yes. He was my lover at one time. (*As Julian averts his head.*) Oh! Perhaps I shouldn't have told you.

32

JULIAN. No, forgive me. Things sometimes . . . are so unexpected. (*Crosses to window seat, sits.*)

MISS ALICE. Yes, they are. I am presently mistress to my lawyer —the gentleman who intimidated you so. He is a pig.

JULIAN. (*Embarrassed.*) Yes, yes. You have . . . never married.

MISS ALICE. (*Quiet amusement.*) Alas.

JULIAN. You are . . . not Catholic.

MISS ALICE. (*The same.*) Again, alas.

JULIAN. No, it is fortunate you are not.

MISS ALICE. I am bored with my present lover.

JULIAN. I . . . (*Shrugs.*)

MISS ALICE. I was not soliciting advice.

JULIAN. (*Quiet laugh.*) Good, for I have none.

MISS ALICE. These six years of yours.

JULIAN. (*Rises, crosses to* D. L. *of ottoman. Says it all in one deep breath.*) There is no mystery to it, my faith in God left me, and I committed myself to an asylum. (*Pause.*) You see? Nothing to it.

MISS ALICE. What an odd place to go to look for one's faith.

JULIAN. You misunderstand me. I did not go there to *look* for my faith, but because *it* had left me.

MISS ALICE. You tell it so easily.

JULIAN. (*Crosses to* C. *Shrugs.*) It is easy to tell.

MISS ALICE. Ah.

JULIAN. (*Giggles a little.*) However, I would not tell your present . . . uh, your lawyer. And that made him quite angry.

MISS ALICE. Have you slept with many women?

JULIAN. (*Carefully.*) I am not certain.

MISS ALICE. (*Tiny laugh.*) It is an easy enough thing to determine.

JULIAN. Not so. For one, I am celibate. A lay brother—you must know—while not a priest, while not ordained, is still required to take vows. And chastity is one of them.

MISS ALICE. A dedicated gesture, to be sure, celibacy without priesthood . . . but a melancholy one, for you're a handsome man . . . in your way.

JULIAN. (*Crosses* L. *above chair, to* U. *of ottoman.*) You're kind.

MISS ALICE. But, tell me: why did you not become a priest? Having gone so far, I should think . . .

JULIAN. A lay brother serves.

33

MISS ALICE. . . . but is not ordained, is more a servant.

JULIAN. The house of God is so grand . . . (*Sweet apologetic smile.*) it needs many servants.

MISS ALICE. How humble. But is that the only reason?

JULIAN. I am not wholly reconciled. Man's God and mine are not . . . close friends.

MISS ALICE. Indeed. But, tell me, how are you not certain that you have slept with a woman?

JULIAN. (*With curiosity. Picks up briefcase.*) Shall I tell you? We have many more important matters. . . .

MISS ALICE. (*Takes briefcase, drops it R. of chair.*) Tell me, please. The money will not run off. Great wealth is patient.

JULIAN. I would not know. Very well. It's good for me, I think, to talk about it. (*Sits on ottoman.*) The institution . . . to which I committed myself—it was deep inland, by the way—was a good one, good enough, and had, as I am told most do, sections—buildings, or floors of buildings—for patients in various conditions . . . some for violent cases, for example, others for children. . . .

MISS ALICE. How sad.

JULIAN. Yes. Well, at any rate . . . sections. Mine . . . my section was for people who were . . . mildly troubled—which I found ironic, for I have never considered the fleeing of faith a mild matter. Nonetheless, for the mildly troubled. The windows were not barred; one was allowed utensils, and one's own clothes. You see, escape was not a matter of urgency, for it was a section for mildly troubled people who had committed themselves, and should escape occur, it was not a danger for the world outside.

MISS ALICE. I understand.

JULIAN. There was a period during my stay, however, when I began to . . . hallucinate, and to withdraw, to a point where I was not entirely certain when my mind was tricking me, or when it was not. (*Rises, steps L. ottoman.*) I believe one would say—how is it said?—that my grasp on reality was . . . tenuous—occasionally. There was, at the same time, in my section, a woman who, on very infrequent occasions, believed that she was the Virgin Mary.

MISS ALICE. (*Mild surprise.*) My goodness.

JULIAN. A quiet woman, plain, but soft features, not hard; at forty, or a year either side, married, her husband the owner of a dry-goods store, if my memory is correct; childless . . . the sort

34

of woman, in short, that one is not aware of passing on the street, or in a hallway . . . unlike you—if you will permit me.

MISS ALICE. (*Smiles.*) It may be I am . . . noticeable, but almost never identified.

JULIAN. You shun publicity.

MISS ALICE. Oh, indeed. And I have few friends . . . that, too, by choice. (*Urges him on with a gesture to sit.*) But please . . .

JULIAN. Of course. My hallucinations . . . (*Sits on ottoman.*) were saddening to me. I suspect I should have been frightened of them—as well as by them—most people are, or would be . . . by hallucinations. But I was . . . saddened. They were, after all, provoked, brought on by the departure of my faith, and this in turn was brought on by the manner in which people mock God. . . .

MISS ALICE. I notice you do not say you lost your faith, but that it abandoned you.

JULIAN. Do I. Perhaps at bottom I had lost it, but I think more that I was confused . . . *and* intimidated . . . by the world about me, and let slip contact with it . . . with my faith. So, I was *sad*dened.

MISS ALICE. Yes.

JULIAN. The periods of hallucination would be announced by a ringing in the ears, which produced, or was accompanied by, a loss of hearing. I would hear people's voices from a great distance and through the roaring of . . . surf. (*Rises, crosses to* D. C.) And my body would feel light, and not mine, and I would float— no, glide.

MISS ALICE. There was no feeling of terror in this? I would be beside myself.

JULIAN. No, as I said, sadness. Aaaaahhh, I would think, I am going from myself again. How very, very sad . . . everything. Loss, great loss.

MISS ALICE. I understand.

JULIAN. And when I was away from myself—never far enough, you know, to . . . blank, just to . . . fog over—when I was away from myself I could not sort out my imaginings from what was real. Oh, sometimes I would say to a nurse or one of the attendants, "Could you tell me, did I preach last night? To the patients? A fire-and-brimstone lesson. Did I do that, or did I imagine it?" And they would tell me, if they knew.

35

MISS ALICE. And did you?

JULIAN. Hm? . . . No, it would seem I did not . . . to their knowledge. But I was never sure, you see.

MISS ALICE. (*Nodding.*) No.

JULIAN. (*A brief, rueful laugh.*) I imagined so many things, or . . . did so many things I thought I had imagined. The uncertainty . . . you know?

MISS ALICE. (*Smiles.*) Are you sure you're not describing what passes for sanity?

JULIAN. (*Laughs briefly, ruefully.*) Perhaps. But one night . . . now, there! You see? I said "one night," and I'm not sure, even now, whether or not this thing happened or, if it did not happen, it did or did not happen at noon, or in the morning, much less at night . . . yet I say night. Doubtless one will do as well as another. So. One *night* the following either happened or did not happen. I was walking in the gardens—or I imagined I was walking in the gardens—walking in the gardens, and I heard a sound . . . sounds from near where a small pool stood, with rosebushes, rather overgrown, a formal garden once, the . . . the place had been an estate, I remember being told. Sounds . . . sobbing? Low cries. And there was, as well, the ringing in my ears, and . . . and fog, a . . . a milkiness, between myself and . . . everything. I went toward the cries, the sounds, and . . . I, I fear my description will become rather . . . vivid now. . . .

MISS ALICE. I am a grown woman.

JULIAN. (*Nods.*) Yes. (*A deep breath. Crosses slowly to* U. *of chair,* L. *of ottoman.*) The . . . the woman, the woman I told you about, who hallucinated, herself, that she was the Virgin . . .

MISS ALICE. Yes, yes.

JULIAN. . . . was . . . was on a grassy space by the pool—or this is what I imagined—on the ground, and she was in her . . . a nightdress, a . . . gossamer, filmy thing, or perhaps she was not, but there she was, on the ground, on an incline, a slight incline, and when she saw me—or sensed me there—she raised her head, and put her arms . . . (*Demonstrates.*) . . . out, in a . . . supplication, and cried, "Help me, help me . . . help me, oh God, God, help me . . . oh, help, help." This, over and over, and with the sounds in her throat between. I . . . I came closer, and the sounds, her sounds, her words, the roaring in my ears, the gossamer and the milk film, I . . . (*Kneels.*) a ROAR, AN OCEAN!

Saliva, perfume, sweat, the taste of blood and rich earth in the mouth, sweet sweaty slipping . . . (*Looks to her apologetically, nods.*) . . . ejaculation. (*She nods.*) The sound cascading away, the rhythms breaking, everything slowly, limpid, quieter, damper, soft . . . soft, quiet . . . done. (*They are both silent. Miss Alice is gripping the arms of her chair, Julian continues softly.*) I have described it to you, as best I can, as it . . . happened, or did not happen.

MISS ALICE. (*Curiously . . . dispassionately.*) I . . . am a very beautiful woman.

JULIAN. (*After a pause which serves as reply to her statement.*) I must tell you more, though. You have asked me for an entirety. (*Rises.*)

MISS ALICE. And a very rich one.

JULIAN. (*Brief pause, nods.*) As I mentioned to you, the woman was given to hallucinations as well, but perhaps I should have said that being the Virgin Mary was merely the strongest of her . . . delusions; she . . . hallucinated . . . as well as the next person, about perfectly mundane matters, too. (*Crosses to D. C.*) So it may be that now we come to coincidence, or it may not. Shortly—several days—after the encounter I have described to you—the encounter which did or did not happen—the woman . . . I do not know which word to use here, either descended or ascended into an ectasy, the substance of which was that she was with child . . . that she was pregnant with the Son of God.

MISS ALICE. And I live here, in all these rooms.

JULIAN. You don't laugh? Well, perhaps you will, at me. I was . . . beside myself, for I assumed the piling of delusion upon delusion, though the chance of there being fact, happening, there somewhere . . . I went to my . . . doctor and told him of my hallucination—if indeed that is what it was. He told me, then . . . that the woman had been examined, that she was suffering from cancer of the womb, that it was advanced, had spread. In a month, she died.

MISS ALICE. Did you believe it?

JULIAN. (*Small smile.*) That she died?

MISS ALICE. That you spoke with your doctor.

JULIAN. (*Pause.*) It has never occurred to me until this moment to doubt it. He has informed me many times.

MISS ALICE. Ah?

37

JULIAN. I *do see* him . . . in reality. We have become friends, we talk from time to time. Socially.

MISS ALICE. Ah. And was it he who discharged you from . . . your asylum?

JULIAN. I was persuaded, eventually, that perhaps I was . . . over-concerned by hallucination; that some was inevitable, and a portion of that—even desirable.

MISS ALICE. Of course.

JULIAN. (*Looking at his hands. Crosses* D. *to* D. L.) Have I answered your question? That I am not . . . sure that I have slept with a woman.

MISS ALICE. (*Puzzling . . . slowly.*) I don't . . . know. Is the memory of something having happened the same as it having happened?

JULIAN. (*Takes out handkerchief.*) It is not the nicest of . . . occurrences—to have described to you.

MISS ALICE. (*Kindly.*) It was many years ago. (*Then, an afterthought.*) Was it not?

JULIAN. Yes, yes, quite a while ago.

MISS ALICE. (*Rises, circles* R. *to* L. *of chair. Vaguely amused.*) I am rich and I am beautiful and I live here in all these rooms . . . without relatives, with a . . . (*Wry.*) companion, from time to time . . . (*Leans forward, whispers, but still amused.*) . . . and with a secret.

JULIAN. Oh? (*Trying to be light, too.*) And may I know it? The secret?

MISS ALICE. I don't know yet.

JULIAN. (*Relaxing.*) Ah-ha.

MISS ALICE. (*Sudden change of mood, to brisk, official, cool. Sits in chair.*) Well then. You're here on business, not for idle conversation, I believe.

JULIAN. (*Confused, even a little hurt.*) Oh . . . yes, that's . . . that's right. (*Sits on ottoman.*)

MISS ALICE. You have instruction to give me—not formal, I'm not about to settle in your faith. Information, facts, questions and answers.

JULIAN. (*Slightly sour.*) Odds and ends, I believe.

MISS ALICE. (*Sharp.*) To you, perhaps. But important if you're to succeed, if you're not to queer the whole business, if you're not to . . .

JULIAN. Yes, yes!

MISS ALICE. So you'll be coming back here . . . when I wish to see you.

JULIAN. Yes.

MISS ALICE. Several times. It might be better if you were to move in. I'll decide it.

JULIAN. Oh . . . well, of course, if you think . . .

MISS ALICE. I think. (*Julian nods acquiescence.*) Very good. No more today, no more now. (*Julian rises, crosses R. of chair, picks up briefcase, crosses R. to doors.*)

JULIAN. (*Up, maybe retreating a little.*) Well, if you'll let me know when . . .

MISS ALICE. (*Rises.*) Come here. (*Julian goes to her at C., she takes his head in her hands, kisses him on the forehead, he registers embarrassment, she laughs, a slightly mocking, unnerving laugh.*) Little recluse. (*Laughs again.*)

JULIAN. (*Crosses R. to door.*) If you'll . . . advise me, or His Eminence, when you'd like me to . . .

MISS ALICE. (*Follows Julian to U. R.*) Little bird, pecking away in the library. (*Laughs again.*)

JULIAN. I'm . . . disappointed you find me so . . . humorous.

MISS ALICE. (*Cheerful, but not contrite.*) Oh, forgive me, I live so alone, the oddest things cheer me up. You . . . cheer me up. (*Moves L. to C. Holds out her hand to be kissed.*) Here. (*Julian hesitates.*) Ah-ah-ah, he who hesitates loses all. (*Julian hesitates again, momentarily, then kisses her hand, but kneeling, as he would kiss a Cardinal's ring. Miss Alice laughs at this.*) Do you think I am a Cardinal? Do I look like a Prince? Have you never even kissed a woman's hand?

JULIAN. (*Back on his feet, evenly.*) No. I have not.

MISS ALICE. (*Kindlier now.*) I'll send for you, we'll have . . . pleasant afternoons, you and I. Goodbye. (*Miss Alice turns away, crosses L. to window, kneels on ottoman with one knee, gazes out a window, her back to the audience. Julian exits R. The Lawyer enters the set from the bedroom door U. R. C.*)

LAWYER. (*Crosses to R. of Miss Alice, a bit abruptly.*) How did it go, eh?

MISS ALICE. (*Turns around, matter-of-factly.*) Not badly.

LAWYER. You took long enough. (*Miss Alice shrugs.*) When are you having him again?

MISS ALICE. (*Very wickedly.*) On business, or privately?

LAWYER. Don't be childish. (*Sits in Miss Alice's chair.*)

MISS ALICE. Whenever you like, whenever you say. (*Seriously.*) Tell me honestly, do you really think we're wise?

LAWYER. Wise? Well, we'll see. If we prove not, I can't think of anything standing in the way that can't be destroyed. (*Pause.*) Can you?

MISS ALICE. (*Rather sadly.*) No. Nothing. (*Rises, crosses L. to mirror.*)

CURTAIN

ACT II

Scene 1

The library—as of Act One, Scene Two. No one on stage. Evening. Miss Alice hurtles through the archway L., half running, half backing, with the Lawyer after her. It is not a chase, she has just broken from him, and her hurtling is the result of sudden freeing.

MISS ALICE. (*Just before and as she is entering, her tone is neither hysterical nor frightened, she is furious and has been mildly hurt. She crosses in to L. of C. doors.*) KEEP . . . GO! GET YOUR . . . LET GO OF ME! (*She is in the room.*) KEEP OFF! KEEP OFF ME!

LAWYER. (*Crosses in, following her. Excited, ruffled, but trying to maintain decorum.*) Don't be hysterical, now.

MISS ALICE. (*Still moving away from him, as he comes on.*) KEEP . . . AWAY. JUST STAY AWAY FROM ME.

LAWYER. I said don't be hysterical.

MISS ALICE. I'll *show* you hysteria. I'll give you *fireworks!* KEEP! Keep away.

LAWYER. (*Soothing, but always moving in on her.*) A simple touch, an affectionate hand on you; nothing more . . .

MISS ALICE. (*Crossing down L. steps. Quiet loathing.*) You're degenerate.

LAWYER. (*Following her. Steely.*) An affectionate hand, in the privacy of a hallway . . .

MISS ALICE. (*Sits in L. C. chair. Almost a shriek.*) THERE ARE PEOPLE!!

LAWYER. Where? There are no people.

MISS ALICE. (*Between her teeth.*) There are people.

LAWYER. (*Feigning surprise.*) There are no people. (*To a child.*) Ahh! (*Walks R. toward the model, indicates it.*) Unless you mean all the little people running around inside here. Is that what you mean?

41

MISS ALICE. (*A mirthless, don't-you-know it laugh.*) Hunh-hunh-hunh-hunh.

LAWYER. Is that who you mean? All the little people in here? (*Crosses L. to Miss Alice. Change of tone to normal, if sarcastic.*) Why don't we show them a few of your tricks, hunh?

MISS ALICE. (*Rises, crosses around chair to R., R. of table, clenched teeth again.*) Keep . . . away . . . from . . . me.

LAWYER. (*Follows her. Without affection.*) To love is to possess, and since I desire to possess you, that must mean conversely that I love you, must it not. Come here. (*Stops u. of table.*)

MISS ALICE. (*With great force.*) PEOPLE!

LAWYER. Your little priest? Your little Julian? He is not . . .

MISS ALICE. He is not a priest!

LAWYER. No. And he is not nearby—momentarily! (*Hissed.*) I am sick of him here day after day, sick of the time you're taking. Will you get it done with!

MISS ALICE. No! (*Lawyer starts to Miss Alice. She crosses L. to L. chair.*) He will be up.

LAWYER. (*Following her.*) Oh, for Christ's sake, he's a connoisseur; he'll be nosing around the goddam wine cellar for hours!

MISS ALICE. (L. *of* L. *chair.*) He will be up. (*Afterthought.*) Butler!

LAWYER. (*Advancing.*) Butler? Let him watch. (*A sneer.*) Which is something I've been meaning to discuss with you for the longest time now. . . .

MISS ALICE. (*Calm, quivering hatred, almost laughing with it.*) I have a loathing for you that I can't describe.

LAWYER. (R. *of* L. *chair.*) You were never one with words. (*Suddenly brutal. Pulls Miss Alice to him.*) NOW, COME HERE.

MISS ALICE. (*Shrugs.*) All right. I won't react, I promise you.

LAWYER. (*Beginning to fondle her.*) Won't react . . . indeed. (*During this next, Miss Alice is backed up against something, and the Lawyer is calmly at her, kissing her neck, fondling her. She is calm, and at first he seems amused.*)

MISS ALICE. What causes this loathing I have for you? It's the way you have, I suppose; the clinical way; methodical, slow . . .

LAWYER. . . . thorough . . .

MISS Alice. . . . uninvolved . . .

LAWYER. . . . oh, very involved . . .

MISS ALICE. . . . impersonality in the most personal things . . .

42

LAWYER. . . . your passivity is exciting . . .

MISS ALICE. . . . passive only to some people . . . (*He nips her ear.*) OW.

LAWYER. A little passion; good.

MISS ALICE. (*As he continues fondling her, perhaps by the end he has her dress off her shoulders.*) With so much . . . many things to loathe, I must choose carefully, to impress you most with it.

LAWYER. Um-humh.

MISS ALICE. Is it the hair? Is it the hair on your back I loathe most? Where the fat lies, on your shoulderblades, the hair on your back . . . black, ugly? . . .

LAWYER. But too short to get a hold on, eh?

MISS ALICE. Is it that—the back hair? It could be; it would be enough. Is it your . . . what is the polite word for it . . . your sex?

LAWYER. (*Mocking.*) Careful now, with a man's pride.

MISS ALICE. Ugly; that too—ugly.

LAWYER. (*Unruffled.*) Better than most, if you care for a man . . .

MISS ALICE. . . . ugly coarse uncut ragged . . . PUSH!

LAWYER. Push . . . yes . . .

MISS ALICE. . . . selfish, hurtful, ALWAYS! OVER AND OVER!

LAWYER. You like it; it feels good. (*Pulls strap off her* L. *shoulder.*)

MISS ALICE. (*Very calm and analytical.*) But is that what I loathe most? It could be; that would be enough, too.

LAWYER. . . . oh, what a list . . .

MISS ALICE. But I think it is most the feel of your skin . . . (*Hard.*) that you can't sweat. (*He stiffens some.*) That your body is as impersonal as your . . . self—dry, uncaring, rubbery . . . dead. (*Lawyer crosses* R. *to* R. C. *chair.*) Ah . . . there . . . that is what I loathe about you most: you're dead. (*Miss Alice sits* L. *chair.*) Moving pushing selfish dry dead. (*Brief pause.*) Does that hurt? Does something finally, beautifully hurt? (*Self-mocking laugh.*) Have I finally gotten . . . into you?

LAWYER. (*A little away from her now.*) Insensitive, still, aren't you, after all this time. Does it hurt? Does something finally hurt?

MISS ALICE. . . . deep, gouging hurt?

LAWYER. (*Crosses around* R. *chair to* C.) Everything! Everything in the day and night, eating, resting, walking, rutting, everything! Everything *hurts*.

MISS ALICE. Awwwwww.

LAWYER. Inside the . . . sensibility, everything hurts. Deeply.

MISS ALICE. (*Ridiculing.*) And is that why I loathe you?

LAWYER. (*A quiet, rueful laugh.*) Probably. (*Crosses* L. *to* L. *of* L. *chair. Quickly back to himself.*) But you, little playmate, you're what I want now. (*Takes her arm.*) GIVE!

MISS ALICE. If Julian comes in here . . .

LAWYER. (*Drops her arm. Shoves her.*) Are you playing it straight, hunh? Or do you like your work a little bit, hunh? (*Again. Pulls her* L. *foot with his own foot.*) Do you enjoy spreading your legs for the clergy? (*Again.*) Hunh?

MISS ALICE. (*Rises, crosses* L. *to sideboard.*) STOP! . . . YOU!

LAWYER. (*Crosses to her.*) Is that our private donation to the Church? Our own grant? YES? (*Grabs her arm, twists it behind her.*) Are we planning to turn into a charitable, educational foundation?

MISS ALICE. (*In pain.*) My arm! (*Butler enters, unnoticed, watches.*)

LAWYER. (*Hard and very serious.*) Don't you dare mess this thing up. You behave the way I've told you; you PLAY-ACT. You do your part; STRAIGHT.

BUTLER. (*Crosses down* R. *steps with tray to table. Calmly.*) Brother Julian . . .

MISS ALICE. Butler! Help me!

BUTLER. . . . has now examined the wine cellar, with awe and much murmuring, and will be with us presently. He's peeing. So I suggest—unless you're doing this for his benefit—uh, you stop. (*Lawyer releases Miss Alice.*)

MISS ALICE. (*As she and the Lawyer pull themselves together. Crosses* R. *to table.*) He hurt me, Butler.

BUTLER. (*Calmly, as if reminding her.*) Often. (*To the Lawyer, with mock friendliness.*) Up to your old tricks, eh?

LAWYER. (*Crossing* R. *to table. Dusting himself off.*) She is . . . not behaving.

BUTLER. (*Very noncommittal.*) Ah me.

MISS ALICE. (*Under her breath, to the Lawyer.*) Savage! (*Realizes. Crosses* R. *to* D. R. *chair, sits.*) Both of you!

44

LAWYER. (*Laughs.*) The maiden in the shark pond.

MISS ALICE. He thinks I'm sleeping with Julian. (*To Lawyer.*) You poor jealous . . .

BUTLER. Are you?

MISS ALICE. (*Indignant.*) No! (*Almost sad about it.*) No, I am not.

LAWYER. She is!

MISS ALICE. I said I am not!

BUTLER. Are you going to?

MISS ALICE. (*After a pause, to Lawyer.*) Am I going to? Am I going to . . . spread my legs for the clergy? Enjoy my work a little? Isn't that what you'd have me do? To not mess it up? To play my part straight? Isn't that what you'll HAVE ME DO?

LAWYER. You don't need urging! . . .

BUTLER. Now, children . . .

MISS ALICE. When the time comes? Won't you have me at him? Like it or not? Well . . . I will like it! (*A little hard breathing from Miss Alice and the Lawyer.*)

BUTLER. (*Picks up keys from tray, crosses* L. *to* C. *Lawyer crosses to* U. *of table.*) Something *should* be done about the wine cellar. I've noticed it—as a passerby would—but Brother Julian pointed out the extent of it to me: bottles have burst, are bursting, corks rotting . . . something to do with the temperature or the dampness. It's a shame, you know.

MISS ALICE. (*Surprisingly shrill.*) Well, fix it!

BUTLER. (*Ignoring her tone.*) Some great years, popping, dribbling away, going to vinegar under our feet. There is a Mouton Rothschild—one I'm especially fond of—that's . . .

LAWYER. (*Pacifying.*) Do. Do . . . fix it.

BUTLER. (*Shakes his head.*) Going. All of it. Great shame.

LAWYER. (*Pours coffee.*) Yes, yes.

BUTLER. (*Brightly.*) Nice thing about having Julian here so much . . . he's helpful. Wines, plants . . . do you know, he told me some astonishing things about ferns. We were in the solarium . . .

MISS ALICE. (*Quiet pleading.*) Please . . . stop.

BUTLER. Oh. Well, it's nice having him about.

LAWYER. (*Sour.*) Oh, we'll be a foursome very soon.

MISS ALICE. (*Brightly.*) Yes.

LAWYER. (*With a mirthless smile.*) Warning.

BUTLER. (*Crosses* L. *to sideboard. Cheerful again.*) It *would* be a great deal more sensible than . . . (*Puts away keys.*) putting out here every day. (*Lawyer picks up coffee.*) We could put him over the chapel! Now, that's a splendid idea. He likes the chapel, he said, not resonant, too small or something, wrong angles, but he likes it . . .

MISS ALICE. When he moves here . . .

LAWYER. (*Crosses to Miss Alice, offers coffee.*) He will move here when I say—and as I say.

MISS ALICE. (*Refuses cup. Fake smile.*) We shall see.

LAWYER. (*Still offhand.*) We shall not see.

JULIAN. (*Offstage. Butler crosses up L. steps. Lawyer crosses to u. of table. Miss Alice crosses to R. C. chair, sits.*) Halloo!

BUTLER. In . . . in here.

MISS ALICE. (*Sotto voce to the Lawyer.*) You say we shall not see? Shall we?

LAWYER. (*As above.*) Warning. (*Julian enters carrying liqueur bottle. Crosses to top of L. steps.*)

JULIAN. Ah! There you all are.

LAWYER. *We* had wondered where *you* were.

MISS ALICE. (*Reminding a child.*) You usually find us here after dinner.

JULIAN. (*Gives liqueur bottle to Butler. Crosses down steps.*) Yes, and a superb dinner.

LAWYER. . . . and then Butler reminded us that you were in the cellar.

JULIAN. (*Crosses R. to Miss Alice. Sincere, but prepared.*) Miss Alice, your . . . home possesses two things that, were I a designer of houses—for the very wealthy, of course—I would put in all my designs. (*Stands L. of Miss Alice.*)

MISS ALICE. (*Smiling.*) And what are they?

LAWYER. (*To Miss Alice, mildly mocking Julian.*) Can't you guess?

MISS ALICE. (*Charmingly.*) Of course I can guess, but I want Julian to have the pleasure of saying it.

JULIAN. A chapel and a wine cellar.

MISS ALICE. (*Agreeing, but is she making light fun?*) Yes.

LAWYER. (*Puts down cup.*) We hear, though, that the wine cellar is a wreck. And aren't there cobwebs in the chapel, too?

JULIAN. (*Light but standing up to him.*) One or two spiders

46

have been busy around the altar, and the organ is . . . in need of use . . .

LAWYER. (*Very funny to him.*) HUNH! (*Julian crosses* R. *of table and pours coffee.*)

JULIAN. (*Choosing to ignore it.*) . . . but it *is* a chapel, a good one. The wine cellar, however . . . (*Shakes his head.*) . . . great, great shame.

BUTLER. Exactly my words.

MISS ALICE. Well, we must have it tended to—and especially since you are our guest so frequently these days, and enjoy good wines.

JULIAN. I would call someone in, a specialist, if I were you.

LAWYER. (*Patronizing.*) Why? Can't you take care of it? Your domain?

JULIAN. (*Quietly.*) The chapel, more, I should think. (*Julian sits in* D. R. *chair. Lawyer crosses* U. C.)

BUTLER. (*Crosses* D. *to sideboard, pours liqueur.*) Where does the Church get its wine . . . for Communion and the like?

JULIAN. Oh, it is grown, made . . . grown, the grapes, harvested, pressed . . . by, by monks.

LAWYER. (*False heartiness.*) A regular profit-making setup, the Church.

JULIAN. (*Quietly, as usual.*) Self-sustaining . . . in some areas.

LAWYER. But not in others, eh? Sometimes the old beggar bell comes out, doesn't it? Priest as leper.

MISS ALICE. (*Mildly to the Lawyer. Butler starts* R. *with tray of liqueur glasses.*) It *is* true: you are not fit for God's sight.

BUTLER. (R. *of Lawyer,* U. R. C. *To the Lawyer, cheerfully interested.*) Is that so? I wasn't sure.

LAWYER. (*To Miss Alice, feigning curiosity and surprise.*) Who whispered it to you?

MISS ALICE. (*Butler gives liqueur to Miss Alice, then Julian. She indicates Julian. Semi-serious.*) My confessor.

LAWYER. (*A sneer, to Julian.*) Did you? And so *you* object, as well? To my mention of the Church as solicitor.

JULIAN. (*Rises, puts down coffee, takes liqueur.*) In England I believe *you* would be referred to as solicitor.

LAWYER. No, I would not. And we are not in England . . . are we?

BUTLER. This place was . . . in England.

47

MISS ALICE. (*Rises, crosses* L. *to* L. *chair, sits. As if suddenly remembering.*) Yes, it was! Every stone, marked and shipped.

JULIAN. (*Crosses to* R. C.) Oh; I had thought it was a replica.

LAWYER. (*Crosses* D. *to Julian.*) Oh no; that would have been too simple. Though it *is* a replica . . . in its way.

JULIAN. Of?

LAWYER. (*Pointing to the model.*) Of that. (*Julian laughs a little, the Lawyer shrugs.*) Ah well. (*Crosses* U. *to model,* L. *of* C.)

JULIAN. (*Crossing to Miss Alice.*) Did your . . . did your father have it . . . put up? (*Miss Alice turns to Lawyer. A parenthesis. Julian crosses to* L. *of* L. *chair.*) It suddenly occurred to me that I know nothing of your family, though I . . . I don't mean to pry. . . .

MISS ALICE. (*A private laugh.*) No, we must not . . . well, should we say that? (*Lawyer crosses* D., R. *of* L. *chair.*) That my father put it up? No. Let us not say that.

BUTLER. (*Crosses* L. *to Lawyer, with liqueur. To Julian, pointing first to the model, then to the room. Lawyer takes liqueur.*) Do you mean the model . . . or the replica?

JULIAN. I mean the . . . I mean . . . what we are in.

BUTLER. *Ah*-ha. And which is that?

JULIAN. That we are in?

BUTLER. Yes.

LAWYER. (*To Julian.*) You are clearly not a Jesuit. (*Turning.*) Butler, you've put him in a clumsy trap.

BUTLER. (*Crosses* R. *to* U. *of table. Shrugging.*) I'm only a servant.

LAWYER. (*To Julian, too sweetly.*) You needn't accept his alternative . . . that since we are clearly not in a model we must be in a replica.

BUTLER. (*Vaguely annoyed.*) Why must he not accept that?

MISS ALICE. Yes. Why not?

LAWYER. I said he did not *need* to accept the alternative. I did not say it was not valid.

JULIAN. (*Cheerfully.*) I will not accept it; the problem is only semantic.

BUTLER. (*Perhaps too consoling.*) Well, yes; that's what I would have thought.

LAWYER. Not necessarily, though. Depends, doesn't it, on your concept of reality, on the limit of possibilities. . . .

48

MISS ALICE. (*Genuinely put off.*) Oh, Lord!

LAWYER. There are no limits to possibi . . . (*Suddenly embarrassed.*) I'm . . . I'm sorry. (*Crosses R. to table, puts down glass.*)

MISS ALICE. (*To Julian, but at the Lawyer.*) He starts in, he will, give him the most sophomoric conundrum, and he'll bore you to death.

LAWYER. (*Turning to Miss Alice. Violently.*) I! Will! Not!

JULIAN. (*To break the silence. Puts glass on sideboard.*) Well . . . perhaps I'm at fault here.

MISS ALICE. (*Quietly, kindly.*) How could you be? . . . Dear Julian.

LAWYER. (*Crosses L. To Miss Alice, burning.*) I thought I had educated you; I thought I had drilled you sufficiently in matters of consequence; (*Growing louder.*) I thought I had made it clear to you the way you were to behave.

JULIAN. Perhaps I should leave now; I think that . . .

LAWYER. DON'T INTERRUPT ME! (*Glares at Julian, who moves off to the model, slowly crossing to U. R., above chair.*)

MISS ALICE. (*To the Lawyer, calmly.*) You forget your place.

LAWYER. (*Crosses to L. of Miss Alice. Clearly trying to get hold of himself.*) I . . . you . . . are quite right . . . Miss Alice, and abstractions *are* upsetting.

MISS ALICE. (*To the Lawyer, patiently.*) Perhaps you'll go home now.

BUTLER. (*Crosses L. to R. of Miss Alice. Cheerfully.*) Shall I have your car brought around?

LAWYER. (*Trying to be private in public.*) I . . . I thought that with so much to attend to, I might . . . spend the night. Of course, if you'd rather I didn't . . . (*Leaves it unfinished. Miss Alice smiles enigmatically.*)

BUTLER. (*Pretending to think the remark was for him.*) I don't mind whether you do or not.

JULIAN. (*At chapel of model. Peering at the model, rather amazed.*) Can it . . . can it be?

LAWYER. In the heat of . . . I, I forgot myself.

MISS ALICE. (*Patronizingly sweet.*) Yes.

LAWYER. (*Matter-of-fact.*) You will forgive me.

MISS ALICE. (*Toying.*) Oh?

BUTLER. Shall I have his car brought around?

LAWYER. (*Kneels. Sudden softening.*) Let me stay.

JULIAN. (*Shy attempt at getting attention.*) Please . . .

MISS ALICE. (*Malicious pleasure in it.*) I don't know . . .

JULIAN. (*More urgently.*) Please!

LAWYER. (*Bitter.*) As you wish, of course. (*Swings his hand back as if to strike her, she flinches.*)

JULIAN. PLEASE!

BUTLER. (*Patiently amused curiosity.*) What is it, for heaven's sake?

JULIAN. (*Pointing to the model.*) The model is . . . on fire; it's on fire!

BUTLER. (*Urgent dropping of butlerish attitudes.*) Where!

LAWYER. Good Christ!

MISS ALICE. Quick! (*The Lawyer and Butler rush u. to the model.*)

BUTLER. *Where*, for Christ's sake!

JULIAN. (*Jostled.*) In the . . . over the . . .

LAWYER. Find it!

BUTLER. (*Peering into various windows with great agitation.*) It's . . . it's the . . . where the hell is it! . . . It's the . . . chapel! The chapel's burning!

MISS ALICE. (*Crosses u. to c. of model, kneels.*) Hurry!

BUTLER. Come on! Let's get to it! (*Begins to run out of the room.*) Are you coming! Julian!

JULIAN. (*Confused, but following.*) But I . . . but . . . yes, of course. (*Julian and Butler cross up R. steps and out R. Lawyer follows, stops on landing.*)

MISS ALICE. (*To the Lawyer as he hangs back.*) We're burning down! Hurry!

LAWYER. (*Crosses c. to Miss Alice, grabs her by the wrist, throws her c., keeps hold.*) Burning down? Consumed? WHY NOT! Remember what I told you. Watch . . . your . . . step! (*He runs out after the others. Miss Alice is left alone, maybe we hear one or two diminishing shouts from the others, offstage. Finally, silence. Miss Alice doesn't rise from the floor, but gradually assumes a more natural position on it.*)

MISS ALICE. (*She alternates between a kind of incantation-prayer and a natural tone. Prayer.*) Let the fire be put out. Let the chapel be saved; let the fire not spread; let us not be consumed. (*Natural.*) He hurt me. My wrist hurts. Who was the boy when

50

I was little hurt my wrist? I don't remember. (*Prayer.*) Let the fire not spread; let them be quick. (*Natural.*) YOU PIG! (*Softly, almost a whine.*) You hurt my wrist. (*Imitates the Lawyer's tone.*) Watch . . . your . . . step. (*Prayer.*) Oh God, I have watched my step. I have . . . trod . . . so carefully. (*Natural and weary.*) Let it all come down—let the whole place . . . go. (*She must now, when using a natural tone, almost give the suggestion of talking to someone in the model. Natural. She rises, crosses* D. R. C.) I don't mean that. I don't remember his name . . . or his face; merely the hurt . . . and that continues, the hurt the same, the name and the face changing, but it doesn't matter. Let them save it. (*Prayer.*) Let them save it. Don't . . . destroy. Let them save the resonance. (*Natural.*) Increase it. Julian says there is no resonance, that it's not right. (*Prayer.*) Let the resonance increase. (*Natural, a little-girl tone. Crosses* D. L. C.) I have tried very hard to be careful, to obey, to withhold my . . . nature? I have tried so hard to be good, but I'm . . . such a stranger . . . here. (*Kneels. Prayer.*) I have tried to obey what I have not understood, understanding that I must obey. Don't destroy! I have tried! TRIED. (*Natural.*) Is that the way about hurt? That *it* does not change . . . but merely its agents? (*Julian appears at* U. C., *unseen by Miss Alice. Natural, still.*) I will hold on. (*Sweetly, apologetically.*) I will try to hold on. (*Prayer.*) I will try to hold on! (*Natural.*) Please, please . . . if you *do* . . . be generous and gentle with me, or . . . just gentle.

JULIAN. (*Softly, a little sadly.*) I don't understand anything. The chapel was in flames. (*Crosses down* R. *steps.*)

MISS ALICE. Yes.

JULIAN. (*At chapel of model.*) . . . and yet . . . I saw the fire here in the model . . . and yet . . . the real chapel was in flames. We put it out. And now the fire here is out as well.

MISS ALICE. (*Preceded by a brief, hysterical laugh.*) . . . yes.

JULIAN. (*Crosses* D. R. C. *Underneath the wonder, some fear.*) I don't understand.

MISS ALICE. (*She is shivering a little.*) It's very hard. Is the chapel saved?

JULIAN. (*His attention on the model.*) Hm? Oh, yes . . . partially, mostly. The . . . the boards, floorboards, around the altar were . . . gave way, were burned through. The altar . . . sank, some, angled down into the burned-through floor. Marble.

MISS ALICE. (*Almost a whisper.*) But the fire is out.

JULIAN. Yes. Out. The spiders, burned to a crisp, I should say, curled-up, burned balls. (*Asking the same question.*) I . . . I don't understand.

MISS ALICE. (*Vaguely to the model.*) It is all well. We are not . . . consumed.

JULIAN. (*Crosses* D. L. *to Miss Alice, kneels.*) Miss Alice? Why, why did it happen that way—in both dimensions?

MISS ALICE. (*Her arms out to him.*) Help me. (*Julian lifts her by the arms, they stand, at arm's length, holding hands, facing each other.*)

JULIAN. Will you . . . tell me anything?

MISS ALICE. (*A helpless laugh, though sad.*) I don't know anything.

JULIAN. But you were . . . (*Stops.*)

MISS ALICE. (*Pleading.*) I don't know anything. (*Julian starts* U. R. *to steps.*)

JULIAN. (*Gently, to placate.*) Very well.

MISS ALICE. (*Miss Alice steps* U., *stopping Julian. Coming closer to him.*) Come stay.

JULIAN. (*Steps* L. *to her.*) Miss Alice?

MISS ALICE. Come stay here. It will . . . be easier. For you.

JULIAN. (*Concern, not anger.*) Did he hurt you?

MISS ALICE. Easier than going back and forth. And for me, too.

JULIAN. Did he?

MISS ALICE. (*After a pause and a sad smile.*) Some. You're shivering, Julian.

JULIAN. No, Miss Alice, it is you . . . you are shivering.

MISS ALICE. The Cardinal will agree to it.

JULIAN. (*Looking toward the model.*) Yes, I . . . suppose so.

MISS ALICE. Are you frightened, Julian?

JULIAN. Why, no, I . . . I am shivering, am I not?

MISS ALICE. Yes.

JULIAN. But I am not . . . yes, I suppose I am . . . frightened.

MISS ALICE. Of what, Julian?

JULIAN. (*Looks toward the model again.*) But there is . . . (*Back.*) . . . of what.

MISS ALICE. Yes.

JULIAN. (*Knowing there is.*) Is there anything to be frightened of, Miss Alice?

MISS ALICE. (*After a long pause.*) Always. (*Julian turns* R.,
steps U. *Miss Alice steps to him.*)

CURTAIN

ACT II

Scene 2

*The library—as of Act One, Scene Two. The Butler is
on stage, sitting on table with book. Phrenological head is
on table. The Lawyer enters* D. L. *immediately, angry,
impatient.*

LAWYER. Well, where are they today?
BUTLER. (*Calm, uninvolved.*) Hm? Who?
LAWYER. (*Crosses* U. C., *flings open doors.*) WHERE IS SHE!
Where is she off to now?
BUTLER. Miss Alice? Well, I don't really know. (*Thinks about
it.*) You look around?
LAWYER. (*Out in hall.*) They're not here.
BUTLER. You don't think they've eloped, do you?
LAWYER. (*Crosses down* R. *steps.*) Do you know!
BUTLER. They're moving together nicely; the fire in the chapel
helped, I thought, though maybe it was intended to . . . brought
them closer.
LAWYER. (L. *of* R. C. *chair.*) Where are they!
BUTLER. They spend so much time together now; everything on
schedule.
LAWYER. (*Takes off coat.*) Where have they gone!
BUTLER. I don't know, really. Out walking? In the gardens?
Driving somewhere? Picnicking, maybe? Cold chicken, cheese, a
Montrachet under an elm? I don't know where they are.
LAWYER. (*Puts coat on back of* R. C. *chair, crosses to sideboard,
gets bottle, pours shot.*) Don't you watch them?
BUTLER. Keep one eye peeled? Can't she take care of herself?
She knows her business. (*Pause, then, quietly meaningful.*) Doesn't
she. (*No answer.*) Doesn't she.

53

LAWYER. (*Crosses* R. *to* R. C. *chair, sits.*) You should watch them. We don't want . . . error. She is . . .

BUTLER. Human? Yes, and clever, too . . . isn't she. *Good* at it, wrapping around fingers, enticing. I recall.

LAWYER. *Too* human; not playing it straight.

BUTLER. Enjoying her work a little? They are not sleeping together yet.

LAWYER. NO! NOT YET!

BUTLER. (*A quiet warning.*) Well, it won't bother you when they do . . . will it.

LAWYER. (*Matter-of-factly.*) I, too: human.

BUTLER. Human, but dedicated.

LAWYER. (*Quiet, sick loathing.*) He doesn't deserve her.

BUTLER. (*Kindly.*) Well, he'll not have her long.

LAWYER. (*Weary.*) No; not long.

BUTLER. On . . . and on . . . we go.

LAWYER. (*Sad.*) Yes.

BUTLER. (*Too offhand, maybe.*) I've noticed, you've let your feelings loose lately; too much: possessiveness, jealousy.

LAWYER. I'm *sorry.*

BUTLER. You used to be so good.

LAWYER. I'm SORRY!

BUTLER. It's all right; just watch it.

LAWYER. Attrition: the toll time takes.

BUTLER. I watch you carefully—you, too—and it's the oddest thing: you're a cruel person, straight through; it's not cover; you're hard and cold, saved by dedication; just that.

LAWYER. (*Soft sarcasm.*) Thank you.

BUTLER. You're welcome, but what's happened is you're acting like the man you wish you were.

LAWYER. Yes?

BUTLER. Feeling things you can't feel. Why don't you mourn for what you are? There's lament enough there.

LAWYER. (*A sad discovery.*) I've never liked you. (*Puts down glass.*)

BUTLER. (*Rises, picks up head. A little sad, too.*) I don't mind. We get along. The three of us.

LAWYER. She's *using* Julian! To humiliate me.

BUTLER. (*Nodding. Crosses to sideboard with head and book. Puts them on sideboard.*) Of course. Humiliate; not hurt. Well, let her do her job the way she wants; she'll lead him, bring him around to it.

LAWYER. But she *cares* for him.

BUTLER. *Of* course; human, a woman. Cares, but it won't get in the way. Let her use what she can. It will be done. Don't you think it's time you went to see His Holiness again?

LAWYER. Eminence, not Holiness. You think it's time I went again? Yes; well, it *is* time. You come, too.

BUTLER. (*Mildly taunting. Puts away bottle.*) But shouldn't I stay here . . . to watch? To fill you in on the goings on? To let you be the last to know?

LAWYER. (*Rises, crosses* U. R. C.) YOU COME! To back me up, when I want emphasis.

BUTLER. In the sense that my father used the word? (*Crosses to* U. *of* L. *chair.*) Wants emphasis: lacks emphasis?

LAWYER. No. The touch of the proletarian: your simplicity, guilelessness . . .

BUTLER. Aw . . .

LAWYER. His Eminence is a pompous ass.

BUTLER. Stupid? I doubt *that.*

LAWYER. Not stupid; an ass.

BUTLER. Cardinals aren't stupid; takes brains to get there; no jokes in the Church.

LAWYER. Pompous!

BUTLER. Well, in front of you, maybe. Maybe has to wear a face; you're not easy. What will you tell him?

LAWYER. What will I tell him? Tell me.

BUTLER. (*Moves* L. *chair to face* D. R. *Lawyer puts on coat-like cape. Butler crosses* L. *of* L. *chair.*) All right. You play Cardinal, I'll play you.

LAWYER. (*Crosses to* L. *chair. Goes into it eagerly, with a laugh.*) Ah, two of you. We are doubly honored. (*Butler starts to kiss ring.*) Will you not sit? (*Lawyer sits* L. *chair.*)

BUTLER. Really? Like that?

LAWYER. And how is our Brother Julian faring . . . in the world of the moneyed and the powerful?

BUTLER. No. Really?

LAWYER. Really! And can we be of service to you, further service?

BUTLER. (*Butler crosses* R. *to* C. *Turns, faces Lawyer.*) Maybe.

55

LAWYER. Maybe? Ah?

BUTLER. Yes, your Brother Julian is going to be taken from you.

LAWYER. Our Brother Julian? Taken? From us? (*Rises.*)

BUTLER. (*Snaps fingers.*) Come on, Your Eminence.

LAWYER. (*Crosses R. of C., past Butler. As the Cardinal again.*) This is a . . . preposterous . . . We . . . we don't understand you.

BUTLER. (*Turns R.*) Isn't the grant enough? Isn't a hundred million a year for twenty years enough? For one man? He's not even a priest.

LAWYER. (*As the Cardinal.*) A man's soul, Sir! (*Himself. Crosses to R. C. chair, puts coat on back.*) Not his soul, mustn't say that to him.

BUTLER. (*Musing. Crosses to L. of L. chair.*) Shall we be dishonest? Well, then, I suppose you'll have to tell him more. Tell him the whole thing.

LAWYER. (*Himself. U. of R. C. chair.*) I will like that. It will blanch his goddamn robes . . . turn 'em white.

BUTLER. (*Chuckles.*) Nice when you can enjoy your work, isn't it? Tell him that Julian is leaving him. That Julian has found what he's after. (*Walks U. C. to the model, indicates it.*) And I suppose you'd better tell him about . . . this, too.

LAWYER. The wonders of the world?

BUTLER. I think he'd better know . . . about this.

LAWYER. Shatter.

BUTLER. (*Sits on model table, L. C.*) And, you know what I think would be a lovely touch?

LAWYER. (*Crosses to Butler. A quiet smile that is also a grimace.*) Tell me.

BUTLER. How eager you are. I think it would be a lovely touch were the Cardinal to marry them, to perform the wedding, to marry Julian to . . .

LAWYER. (*Looks at chapel.*) Alice.

BUTLER. Miss Alice.

LAWYER. (*To Butler.*) Alice!

BUTLER. Well, all right; one through the other. But have him marry them.

LAWYER. (*Smiles a little.*) It would be nice.

BUTLER. I thought so.

LAWYER. (*Crosses D. L.*) But shall we tell him the whole thing? The Cardinal? What is happening?

BUTLER. (*Crosses R. to L. of table.*) How much can he take?

LAWYER. He is a man of God, however much he simplifies, however much he worships the symbol and not the substance.

BUTLER. Like everyone.

LAWYER. Like most. (*Sits L. chair.*)

BUTLER. Julian can't stand that; he told me so: men make God in their own image, he said. (*Sits on table.*) Those six years I told you about.

LAWYER. Yes. When he went into an asylum. YES.

BUTLER. It was—because he could not stand it, wasn't it? The use men put God to.

LAWYER. It's perfect; wonderful.

BUTLER. Could not reconcile.

LAWYER. No.

BUTLER. God as older brother, scout leader, couldn't take that.

LAWYER. And still not reconciled.

BUTLER. Has pardoned men, I think. Is walking on the edge of an abyss, but is balancing. Can be pushed . . . over, back to the asylums.

LAWYER. (*Butler turns R. Smooths table cloth.*) Or over . . . to the Truth. (*Addressing Julian, as if he were there, some thunder in the voice. Turns to audience.*) God, Julian? Yes? God? Whose God? Have you pardoned men their blasphemy, Julian? Have you forgiven them?

BUTLER. (*Rises. Quiet echoing answers, being Julian.*) No, I have not, have not really; have let them, but cannot accept.

LAWYER. Have not forgiven. No, Julian. Could you ever?

BUTLER. (*Ibid.*) It is their comfort; my agony. (*Sits R. C. chair.*)

LAWYER. (*Rises, crosses C.*) Soft God? The servant? Gingerbread God with the raisin eyes?

BUTLER. (*Ibid.*) I cannot accept it.

LAWYER. Then don't accept it, Julian.

BUTLER. But there is something. There is a true God.

LAWYER. There is an abstraction, Julian, but it cannot be understood. You cannot worship it.

BUTLER. (*Ibid.*) There is more.

LAWYER. There is Alice, Julian. That can be understood. Only the mouse in the model. Just that.

BUTLER. (*Ibid.*) There must be more.

LAWYER. The mouse. Believe it. Don't personify the abstraction, Julian, limit it, demean it. Only the mouse, the toy. And that does not exist . . . but is all that can be worshiped. (*Backing* L. *to* L. *of* L. *chair.*) . . . Cut off from it, Julian, ease yourself, ease off. No trouble now; accept it.

BUTLER. (*Rises, crosses* D. R. *Talking to Julian now.*) Accept it, Julian; ease off. Worship it . . .

LAWYER. Accept it.

BUTLER. (*After a pause, normal again.*) Poor, poor Julian.

LAWYER. (*Normal, too.*) He can make it.

BUTLER. I hope he can.

LAWYER. If not? (*Shrugs.*) Out with him.

BUTLER. (*Pause.*) You cannot tell the Cardinal . . . that.

LAWYER. (*Weary.*) The benefits to the Church.

BUTLER. Not simply that.

LAWYER. And a man's soul. If it be saved . . . what matter how?

BUTLER. (*Crosses* L., *picks up Lawyer's coat, gives to Lawyer at* C. *Picks up own coat from* L. *banister, crosses up* L. *steps.*) Then we'd best go to him.

LAWYER. Yes.

BUTLER. Leave Julian to Miss Alice; he is in good hands.

LAWYER. (*Crosses up* R. *steps. Quiet, sick rage rising.*) But his hands . . . on her.

BUTLER. (*Soothing.*) Temporary . . . temporal. You'll have her back.

LAWYER. All right.

BUTLER. (*Crosses out* R.) Let's go.

LAWYER. (*Turns to the model, addresses it, quietly, but forcefully, no sarcasm.*) Rest easy; you'll have him. . . . Hum; purr; breathe; rest. You will have your Julian. Wait for him. He will be yours. (*Crosses out* R.)

CURTAIN

ACT II

Scene 3

Miss Alice's sitting room, as of Act One, Scene Three. Julian is on stage, near the fireplace, carries a riding crop, the door to the bedroom is ajar.

JULIAN. (*At window, foot on window seat. After a moment, over his shoulder.*) It was fun, Miss Alice; it was fun. (*Crosses* D.)

MISS ALICE. (*From behind the door.*) What, Julian?

JULIAN. (*Turns* U. *to door.*) It was . . . I enjoyed it; very much.

MISS ALICE. (*Her head appearing from behind the door.*) Enjoyed what?

JULIAN. (*Turns away.*) Riding; it was . . . exhilarating.

MISS ALICE. I would never have thought you rode. You were good. (*Disappears.*)

JULIAN. (*A small, self-deprecating laugh.*) Oh. Yes. When I was young—a child—I knew a family who . . . kept horses, as a pastime, not as a business. They were moneyed—well, had *some*. It was one of their sons who was my playmate . . . and we would ride.

MISS ALICE. (*Still behind the door.*) Yes.

JULIAN. You remember, you know how seriously children talk, the cabalas we have . . . had. (*Crosses* D. L.) My friend and I would take two hunters, and we would go off for hours, and talk ourselves into quite a state— (*Sits on ottoman.*) mutually mesmerizing, almost an hysteria. We would forget the time, and bring the animals back quite lathered. (*Laughs.*) We would be scolded —no: cursed out—by one groom or another; usually by a great dark Welshman—a young fellow who always scowled and had— I remember it clearly, for I found it remarkable— (*Rises, crosses* U. C.) the hairiest hands I have ever seen, with hair—and this is what I found most remarkable—tufts of coarse black hair on his thumbs. (*Looks at his own thumbs.*) Not down, or a few hairs, which many of us have, but tufts. This Welshman.

MISS ALICE. (*Comes into room, wearing a black negligee with great sleeves.*) D. H. Lawrence.

JULIAN. Pardon?

59

MISS ALICE. (*Closes door.*) "Love on the Farm." Don't you
know it? (*Circles him to L. as she recites it, mock-stalks him.*)
> "I hear his hand on the latch, and rise from my chair
> Watching the door open . . .
> He flings the rabbit soft on the table board
> And comes toward me: he! the uplifted sword
> Of his hand against my bosom! . . .
> . . . With his hand he turns my face to him
> And caresses me with his fingers that still smell grim
> Of rabbit's fur! . . .
> And down his mouth comes on my mouth! and down
> His bright dark eyes over me . . .
> . . . his lips meet mine, and a flood
> Of sweet fire sweeps across me, so I drown
> Against him, die and find death good!"

(*Cocks her head, smiles.*) No?
JULIAN. (*Embarrassed.*) That was . . . not quite my reaction.
MISS ALICE. (*Crosses to chair. A great, crystal laugh.*) No!
Silly Julian! No. (*Conspiratorial.*) That was a verse I knew at
school, that I memorized. "And down his mouth comes on my
mouth." Oh! That would excite us so . . . at school; (*Sits in
chair.*) things like that. (*Normal tone, a shrug, a smile.*) Early
eroticism; mental sex play.
JULIAN. (*Still embarrassed. Crosses L. to window seat.*) Yes.
MISS ALICE. I've embarrassed you!
JULIAN. No! No!
MISS ALICE. Poor Julian; I have. And you were telling me about
horseback riding.
JULIAN. (*Sits on window seat.*) No, I was telling you about the
groom, as far as that goes. And I suppose . . . yes, I suppose . . .
those thumbs were . . . erotic for *me*—at that time, if you think
about it; mental sex play. Unconscious.
MISS ALICE. (*Sweetly, to divert him.*) It *was* fun riding. *Today.*
JULIAN. Yes!
MISS ALICE. I am fond of hair—man's body hair, except that on
the back. (*Very offhand.*) Are you hairy, Julian?
JULIAN. I . . . my chest is rather nice, but my arms are . . .
surprisingly hairless.
MISS ALICE. And you have no back hair.

JULIAN. (*Rises, steps to* C.) Well . . . do you really wish to know?

MISS ALICE. (*With a laugh.*) Yes!

JULIAN. (*Nods in acquiescence.*) I have no . . . back hair, in the usual sense—of the shoulders . . . (*Miss Alice nods.*) . . . but there is hair, at the small of the back . . . rising.

MISS ALICE. Yes, yes, well, *that* is nice. (*Laughs, points to the crop.*) You're carrying the crop. Are you still in the saddle?

JULIAN. (*Laughing, shyly brandishing the crop. Crosses to ottoman.*) Are you one of Mr. Lawrence's ladies? Do you like the smell of saddle soap, and shall I take my crop to you? (*Puts foot on ottoman.*)

MISS ALICE. (*Rises, kneels on ottoman. Briefest pause, testing.*) Would you?

JULIAN. (*Crosses to* L. *Halfhearted laugh.*) MISS ALICE!

MISS ALICE. Nobody does things naturally any more—so few people have the grace. A man takes a whip to you—a loving whip, you understand—and you *know*, deep and sadly, that it's imitation —literary, seen. (*Intentionally too much.*) No one has the natural graces any more.

JULIAN. (*Turns, whip gesture. Crosses to window seat, puts the crop down, quietly.*) I have . . . not whipped . . .

MISS ALICE. But surely you have.

JULIAN. (*Sits on window seat. An apology.*) I do not recall.

MISS ALICE. (*Crosses* L. *to Julian. Expansive.*) Oh, my Julian! How many layers! Yes?

JULIAN. We . . . simplify our life . . . as we grow older.

MISS ALICE. (*Teasing him.*) But from understanding and acceptance; not from . . . emptying ourselves.

JULIAN. There are many ways.

MISS ALICE. (*Crosses* D. *and then* U. *Showing her outfit.*) Do you like this?

JULIAN. (*Rises.*) It is most . . . becoming.

MISS ALICE. (*Stands by Julian. Giggles.*) We're dressed quite alike.

JULIAN. (*Crosses* C. *He, too.*) But the effect is not the same.

MISS ALICE. No. It *is* easier for you living here . . . isn't it?

JULIAN. It's . . . more than a person could want—or *should* want, which is something we must discuss.

MISS ALICE. (*Sensing a coming disappointment.*) Oh . . .

JULIAN. Really.

MISS ALICE. (*Not pleasantly.*) What do we do wrong?

JULIAN. One of the sins is gluttony . . .

MISS ALICE. Are you getting a belly?

JULIAN. (*Smiles, but won't be put off.*) . . . and it has many faces—or many bellies, if you wish. It's a commonplace that we can have too much of things, and I have too much . . . of comfort, of surroundings, of ease, of kindness . . . of happiness. I am filled to bursting.

MISS ALICE. (*Steps in. Hard.*) I think perhaps you misunderstand why you're here. You're *not* here to . . . to indulge yourself, to . . .

JULIAN. (*Tight-lipped.*) I'm aware of that.

MISS ALICE. . . . to . . . to ease in. You're here in service to your Church.

JULIAN. I've not lost sight of my function.

MISS ALICE. I wonder!

JULIAN. (*Really quite angry.*) And *I* wonder! What's being *done* to me. Am I . . . am I being temp—tested in some fashion?

MISS ALICE. (*Jumping on it.*) Tempted?

JULIAN. Tested in some fashion?

MISS ALICE. TEMPTED?

JULIAN. BOTH! Tested! What! My . . . my sincerity, my . . . my other cheek? You have allowed that . . . that *man,* your . . . your lover, to . . . ridicule me. You have permitted it.

MISS ALICE. I? Permit?

JULIAN. You have allowed him to abuse me, my position, his, the Church; you have tolerated it, and *smiled.*

MISS ALICE. Tolerate!

JULIAN. And smiled. WHY AM I BEING TESTED! . . . And why am I being tempted? By luxury, by ease, by . . . content . . . by things I do not care to discuss. (*Crosses away,* R.)

MISS ALICE. (*Unsympathetic.*) You're answerable to your own temptations.

JULIAN. (*At* U. R.) Yes?

MISS ALICE. (*Singsong and patronizing.*) Or God is. (*Julian snorts.*) No? God is not? Is not answerable?

JULIAN. (*Crosses to her.*) Knows. But is not answerable. I.

MISS ALICE. (*Softening some.*) Then *be* answerable.

JULIAN. To my temptations, I am. (*To himself more than to her.*)

62

It would be so easy to . . . fall in, to . . . accept these surroundings. Oh, life would speed by!

MISS ALICE. With all the ridicule?

JULIAN. That aside.

MISS ALICE. You *have* a friend here . . . as they put it.

JULIAN. (*Smiles.*) Butler. Yes; he's nice.

MISS ALICE. (*A little laugh.*) I meant me.

JULIAN. Well, of *course*. . . .

MISS ALICE. Or, do you think of me otherwise? (*Julian crosses* D. L.) Do *I* tempt you?

JULIAN. You, Miss Alice?

MISS ALICE. Or, is it merely the fact of temptation that upsets you so?

JULIAN. I have longed . . . to be of great service. When I was young—and very prideful—I was filled with a self-importance that was . . . well disguised. Serve. (*Crosses* U. C. *Miss Alice counters* L.) That was the active word: I would serve! (*Clenches his fist.*) I would serve, and damn anyone or anything that stood in my way. I would shout my humility from the roof and break whatever rules impeded my headlong rush toward obedience. I suspect that had I joined the Trappist order, where silence is the law, I would have chattered about it endlessly. I was impatient with God's agents, and with God, too, I see it now. A . . . novice porter, ripping suitcases from patrons' hands, cursing those who preferred to carry some small parcel for their own. (*Crosses* D. R.) And I was blind to my pride, and intolerant of any who did not see me as the humblest of men. (*Sits in chair.*)

MISS ALICE. (*A little malice. Claps, steps to* C.) You phrase it so; I suspect you've said it before.

JULIAN. Doubtless I have. Articulate men often carry set paragraphs.

MISS ALICE. (*Crosses* R.) Pride still.

JULIAN. Some.

MISS ALICE. And how did your ambition sit?

JULIAN. Ambition? Was it? (*Miss Alice displays a knee casually; Julian jumps.*) What are you doing!

MISS ALICE. (*Vague flirting.*) I'm . . . sorry. (*She covers her knee.*)

JULIAN. (*Rises, crosses* C.) Well. Ambition, yes, I suppose—ambition to be nothing, to be least. Most obedient, humblest. How did it sit? For some, patiently, but not well. For me? Even less well. But I . . . learned.

MISS ALICE. To . . . subside. Is that the simplification you mentioned before? Of your life. To subside . . . and vanish; to leave no memory.

JULIAN. No; I wish to leave a . . . memory—of work, of things done. I've told you; I wish to be of great service, to move great events; but when it's all time for crediting, I'd like someone to say no more than "Ah, wasn't there someone involved in this, who brought it all about? A priest? Ah-ha, a *lay* brother—was that it." (*Smiles.*) Like that. The memory of someone who helped.

MISS ALICE. (*Pauses, then laughs.*) You're lying!

JULIAN. I? (*Then they both laugh, like conspiratorial children.*)

MISS ALICE. Every monster was a man first, Julian; every dictator was a colonel who vowed to retire once the revolution was done; it's so easy to postpone elections, little brother.

JULIAN. The history of the Church . . .

MISS ALICE. The history of the Church shows half its saints were martyrs, martyred either for the Church, or by it. (*Julian crosses u. to window seat.*) The chronology is jammed with death-seekers and hysterics: the bloodbath to immortality, Julian. Joan was only one of the suicides.

JULIAN. (*Quivering with intensity. Sits on window seat.*) I WISH TO SERVE AND . . . BE FORGOTTEN.

MISS ALICE. (*Comes over, strokes his cheek.*) Perhaps you will, Julian. (*He takes her hand, kisses it, puts it back on his cheek.*) Yes?

JULIAN. (*Guiltily.*) I wish to be of service. (*A little giggle.*) I *do.*

MISS ALICE. And be forgotten.

JULIAN. Yes.

MISS ALICE. (*Stroking his head.*) Not even remembered a little? By some? As a gentle man, gentle Julian . . .

JULIAN. Per . . . perhaps.

MISS ALICE. . . . my little lay brother and expert on wines; my little horseback rider and crop switcher . . .

JULIAN. (*As she ruffles his hair.*) Don't . . . do that.

MISS ALICE. (*Ruffles harder.*) My little whipper, and RAPIST?

JULIAN. (*Rising, moving away to* C.) DON'T!

MISS ALICE. (*Pouting, advancing.*) Julian . . .

64

JULIAN. No, now; no.

MISS ALICE. (*Still pouting.*) Julian, come kiss me.

JULIAN. Please!

MISS ALICE. (*Singsong.*) Come kiss.

JULIAN. (*A plea.*) Miss Alice . . . Just . . . let me do my service, and let me go. (*Turns R., starts R.*)

MISS ALICE. (*Abruptly to business, not curt, though.*) But you're doing great service. Not many people have been put in the position you've been graced by—not many. Who knows—had some lesser man that you come, some bishop, all dried and salted, clacketing phrases from memory, or . . . one of those insinuating super-salesmen your Church uses, had one of them come . . . who knows? Perhaps the whole deal would have gone out the window.

JULIAN. (*Crosses to her.*) Surely, Miss Alice, you haven't been playing games with . . . so monumental a matter.

MISS ALICE. The rich are said to be quixotic, the very wealthy cruel, overbearing; who is to say—might not vast wealth, the insulation of it, make one quite mad? Games? (*Steps in to Julian.*) Oh, no, my little Julian, there are no games played here; this is for keeps, and in dead earnest. There *are* cruelties, for the insulation breeds a strange kind of voyeurism; and there is impatience, too, over the need to accomplish what should not be explained; and, at the end of it, a madness of sorts . . . but a triumph.

JULIAN. (*Hands apart.*) Use me, then . . . for the triumph.

MISS ALICE. (*Moving on him again.*) You are *being* used, my little Julian. *I* am being used . . . my little Julian. You want to be . . . employed, do you not? Sacrificed, even?

JULIAN. I have . . . there are no secrets from you, Miss Alice . . . I have . . . dreamed of sacrifice.

MISS ALICE. (*She touches his neck.*) Tell me.

JULIAN. You mustn't do . ·. . it is not wise . . .

MISS ALICE. Tell me. (*She will circle him, touch him occasionally, kiss the back of his neck once during the next speech.*)

JULIAN. Still my pride . . . a vestige of it. (*He becomes quite by himself during this, unaware of her. He sits on ottoman. She is U. L. of ottoman.*) Oh, when I was still a child, and read of the Romans, how they used the saints as playthings—enraged children gutting their teddy bears, dashing the head of their doll against the bedpost, I could . . . I could entrance myself, and

65

see the gladiator on me, his trident fork against my neck, and hear, even hear, as much as feel, the prongs as they entered me; the . . . the beast's saliva dripping from the yellow teeth, the slack sides of the mouth, the . . . sweet, warm breath of the lion; great paws on my spread arms . . . even the rough leather of the pads; and to the point of . . . as the great mouth opened, the breath no longer warm but hot, the fangs on my jaw and forehead, positioned . . . IN. And as the fangs sank in, the great tongue on my cheek and eye, the splitting of the bone, and the *blood* . . . just before the great sound, the coming dark and the silence. I could . . . experience it all. And was . . . engulfed. (*A brief laugh, but not breaking the trance.*) Oh, martyrdom. To be that. To be able . . . to be that.

MISS ALICE. (*Softly, into his ear, he does not hear it.*) Marry me, Julian.

JULIAN. The . . . death of the saints . . . was always the beginning of their lives. To go bloodstained and worthy . . . upward. I could feel the blood on my robes as I went; the smell of the blood, as intense as paint . . . and warm . . . and painless.

MISS ALICE. Marry me.

JULIAN. "Here. I have come. You see my robes? They're red, are they not? Warm? And are not the folds caught together . . . as the blood coagulates? The . . . fingers of my left hand—of both!—are . . . are hard to move apart, as the blood holds finger to finger. (*Miss Alice crosses* u. *of ottoman to chair.*) And there is a wound in me, the warm dark flow . . . runs down my belly . . . to . . . bathing my groin. You see? I have come . . . bloodstained and worthy."

MISS ALICE. Marry me.

JULIAN. (*Still self-tranced.*) Bathed. . . my groin. And as the thumbs of the gladiator pressed . . . against . . . my neck, I . . . as the lion's belly pressed on my chest, I . . . as the . . . I . . . or as the woman sank . . . on the mossy hillock by the roses, and the roar is the crunching growl is the moan is the sweat-breathing is the . . .

MISS ALICE. (*Behind him, her arms around his neck, on his chest.*) . . . sweat-breathing on the mossy hillock and the white mist in the perfumes . . .

JULIAN. . . . fumes . . . lying . . . on the moss hill in the white filmy gladiator's belly pressing on the chest fanged and the

66

soft hard tongue and the *blood* (*She holds his hand.*) . . . ENTERS
. . . (*Lurches from the ottoman.*) . . . STOP! . . . THAT! (*He backs to* C. *and* U.)

MISS ALICE. (*Coming at him slowly, circling to* C.) Come to
Alice, Julian, in your sacrifice . . .

JULIAN. (*Moving away, but helpless.*) Stay . . . away . . .
stay.

MISS ALICE. . . . give yourself to her, Julian . . .

JULIAN. . . . a . . . away . . .

MISS ALICE. (*Sweetly singsong.*) Come marry Alice, she wants
you so; she says she wants you so, come give yourself to Alice;
oh, Alice needs you and your sacrifice . . .

JULIAN. . . . no . . . no . . .

MISS ALICE. . . . Alice says she wants you, come to Alice, Alice
tells me so, she wants you, come to Alice . . .

JULIAN. . . . no . . . sacrifice . . .

MISS ALICE. Alice tells me so, instructs me, come to her. (*Miss
Alice has her back to the audience, Julian facing her, but at a
distance, she takes her gown and, spreading her arms slowly, opens
the gown wide, it is the unfurling of great wings.*)

JULIAN. (*Shaking, staring at her body.*) . . . and . . . sacrifice
. . . on the altar of . . .

MISS ALICE. Come . . . come . . .

JULIAN. . . . the . . . Lord . . . God . . . in . . . Heaven . . .

MISS ALICE. Come . . . (*Julian utters a sort of dying cry and
moves, his arms in front of him, to Miss Alice, when he reaches
her, she enfolds him in her great wings. Soothing.*) You will be
hers; you will sacrifice yourself to her . . .

JULIAN. (*Muffled.*) Oh my God in heaven . . .

MISS ALICE. (*Her head going back, calling out.*) Alice! . . .
Alice? . . .

JULIAN. (*Slowly kneeling within the great wings.*) . . . in . . .
my . . . sacrifice . . .

MISS ALICE. (*Still calling out.*) He will be yours! He will be
yours! AAAAALLLLLIIIIICCCCCEEEEE!

CURTAIN

ACT III

*The library, as of Act One, Scene Two. No one on stage.
After a moment or so, Butler enters* U. C. *and goes down*
L. *steps, carrying what looks to be a pile of gray sheets.
They are clearly quite heavy. He sets them down on a
table* R., *straightens his shoulders from the effort, looks
at various chairs, turns to counting the pile. Julian enters*
U. C., *at more than a casual pace, dressed in a suit.*

JULIAN. Butler!

BUTLER. (*Deliberate pause, then.*) . . . four . . . five . . .
(*Pretending suddenly to see Julian.*) Oh! Hello there.

JULIAN. Where . . . I . . . I feel quite *lost.*

BUTLER. (*No comment.*) Why?

JULIAN. (*Agitation underneath. Butler puts sheet down on* U. R.
chair.) Well, uh . . . I will confess I haven't participated in . . .
been married before, but . . . I can't imagine it's usual for everyone to disappear.

BUTLER. (*Puts sheet down on* D. R. *chair.*) Has everyone?

JULIAN. Yes! (*Quieter.*) Yes, I . . . per—perhaps His Eminence
is occupied, or has business— (*Julian crosses down* R., *steps to
table. Butler crosses* L. *to* L. *chair, puts sheet on back.*) that's it!
—has business with . . . but—but why *she* should . . . There I
was . . . one moment married, flooded with white, and . . . then
. . . the next, alone. Quite alone, in the . . . echoes.

BUTLER. There is an echo, sometimes, all through it, down every
long hall, up in the huge beams . . .

JULIAN. But to be left alone!

BUTLER. (*Crosses* D. L. C.) Aren't you used to that?

JULIAN. (*Sits in* R. C. *chair.*) Suddenly!

BUTLER. (*Sad smile.*) Like a little boy? When the closet door
swings shut after him? Locking him in the dark?

JULIAN. Hm? Yes . . . yes, like that. (*Shudders a little.*) Ter-
rifying.

68

BUTLER. And it's always remote, an attic closet, where one should not have been, where no one can hear, and is not likely to come . . . for a very long time.

JULIAN. (*Asking him to stop.*) Yes!

BUTLER. (*To the sheets again counting them.*) We learn so early . . . are *told*, where not to go, the things we should not do. And there's often a reason.

JULIAN. (*Rises.*) And *she* vanished as well.

BUTLER. (*Crosses to L. chair.*) Who?

JULIAN. My . . . my wife.

BUTLER. And who is that?

JULIAN. (*Crosses to Butler. As if Butler had forgotten everything.*) Miss Alice!

BUTLER. Ah. Really?

JULIAN. Butler, you saw the wedding!

BUTLER. (*Puzzles it a moment.*) Quite so; I did. We . . . Well. (*Crosses to R. C. chair.*) Perhaps Miss Alice is changing.

JULIAN. She *must* be; of course. But . . . for everyone to . . . vanish, as if I'd turned my back for a *moment*, and an hour elapsed, or a . . . dimension had . . .

BUTLER. (*At U. R. chair. Passing it over.*) Yes, a dimension—well, that happens.

JULIAN. (*Still preoccupied.*) Yes, she must be . . . upstairs. (*Sees Butler smoothing sheets.*) What . . . what are you doing?

BUTLER. What?

JULIAN. What are those?

BUTLER. (*At D. R. chair.*) These? (*Looks at them.*) Uh . . . sheets, or covers, more accurately.

JULIAN. (*Still quite nervous, staying away.*) What are they for?

BUTLER. To . . . cover.

JULIAN. (*Ibid.*) Cover *what!*

BUTLER. Oh . . . nothing; no matter. Housework, that's all. One of my labors.

JULIAN. (*Crosses L. of L. chair.*) I . . . I would have thought you'd have champagne . . . ready, that you'd be busy with the party. . . .

BUTLER. (*Crosses to L. of table.*) One does *many* things. You'll have your champagne, sir, never fear.

JULIAN. I'm sorry; I . . . I was so upset.

BUTLER. Yes.

JULIAN. (*Attempting a joke.*) After all, I've not been married before.
BUTLER. No.
JULIAN. And the procedures are a little . . . well, you know.
BUTLER. Yes.
JULIAN. (*Starts to cross to L. chair. Is stopped by Butler's look.*) . . . still . . .
BUTLER. Yes.
JULIAN. (*Crosses U. of L. chair.*) It all *does* seem odd.
BUTLER. (*Sits on edge of table.*) Marriage is a confusing business.
JULIAN. Have . . . have you been . . . married? (*Butler gives a noncommittal laugh as answer. Julian crosses R. to C.*) I . . . I don't know if marriage is, but certainly the circumstances surrounding this *wedding* are rather . . .
BUTLER. (*A fairly chilling smile.*) Special people, special problems.
JULIAN. (*Hurt.*) Oh. Well . . . yes.
BUTLER. (*Disdainful curiosity.*) Do you . . . *feel* married?
JULIAN. (*Withdrawn.*) Not having been, I cannot say. (*Pause.*) Can I?
BUTLER. No. I suppose not.
JULIAN. (*Crosses to Butler.*) No. I wonder if . . . I wonder if you could go upstairs, perhaps, and see if Miss Alice . . . my *wife* . . . is . . .
BUTLER. (*Rises.*) No. (*Then, rather stern.*) I have much too much work to do. (*Cheerful.*) I'll get you some champagne, though. (*Crosses up R. steps to U. C.*)
JULIAN. (*At R. of R. C. chair. Rather removed.*) No, I'll . . . wait for the others, if they haven't all . . . disappeared.
BUTLER. (*Noncommittal.*) To leave you alone with your bride, on your wedding night? No; not yet.
JULIAN. (*For something to say, as much as anything, yet hopeful of an answer, or an explanation. Sits R. C. chair.*) Miss Alice . . . chose not to invite . . . friends . . . to the ceremony.
BUTLER. (*Chuckle.*) Ah, no. Alice . . . (*Julian looks at him.*) *Miss* Alice does not have friends; (*Crosses L. to globe.*) admirers, yes. Worshipers . . . but not buddies.
JULIAN. (*Puzzled.*) I asked her why she had not, and she replied . . .

70

BUTLER. (*Improvising.*) . . . it is you, Julian, who are being married . . . ?

JULIAN. (*Too self-absorbed to be surprised.*) Yes; something like that.

BUTLER. Your wife is . . . something of a recluse.

JULIAN. (*Hopeful.*) But so outgoing!

BUTLER. Yes? Well, then; you will indeed have fun. (*Crosses down* L. *steps to* L. *chair. Mock instructions.*) Uncover the chandeliers in the ballroom! Lay on some footmen! Unplug the fountains! Trim the maze!

JULIAN. (*More or less to himself.*) She must have friends . . . (*Unsure.*) must she not?

BUTLER. (*Stage whisper.*) I don't know; no one has ever asked her.

JULIAN. (*Laughing nervously.*) Oh, indeed! (*Miss Alice comes hurriedly into the room from* L.; *she has on a suit. She sees only Butler first.*)

MISS ALICE. Butler! Have you seen . . . ? (*Sees Julian.*) Oh, I'm . . . sorry. (*She begins to leave, crossing up* L. *steps to* U. C.)

JULIAN. (*Rises, crosses* U. C.) There ·you are. No, wait; wait! (*But Miss Alice has left the room. In need of help.*) I find everything today puzzling.

BUTLER. (*Crosses towards Julian. About to give advice.*) Look . . . (*Thinks better of it.*)

JULIAN. Yes?

BUTLER. (*Shrugs.*) Nothing. (*Crosses* D. L. C.) The wages of a wedding day.

JULIAN. (*Crosses* D. *to Butler.*) Are you my friend?

BUTLER. (*Takes a while to think about the answer.*) I am, yes; but you'll probably think not.

JULIAN. Is something being kept from me?

BUTLER. (*Turns to Julian. After a pause.*) You loathe sham, do you not?

JULIAN. Yes.

BUTLER. As do we all . . . most of us. You are dedicated to the reality of things, rather than their appearance, are you not?

JULIAN. Deeply.

BUTLER. As are . . . some of us.

JULIAN. It was why I retreated . . . withdrew . . . to the asylum.

71

BUTLER. Yes, yes. And you are devout.

JULIAN. You know that.

BUTLER. When you're locked in the attic, Julian, in the attic closet, in the dark, do you care who comes?

JULIAN. (*Steps back.*) No. But . . .

BUTLER. (*Starts to leave, crossing* L.) Let me get the champagne.

JULIAN. Please!

BUTLER. So that we all can toast. (*Crosses up* L. *steps. As Butler leaves, the Cardinal enters from* U. C., *goes down* R. *steps to* C.) Ah! Here comes the Church. (*Butler stops on* U. C. *platform.*)

JULIAN. (*Going to the Cardinal, kneeling before him, kissing his ring, holding the ring hand afterward, staying kneeling.*) Your Eminence.

CARDINAL. Julian. Our dear Julian. (*Julian rises.*)

BUTLER. Have you caught the bride?

CARDINAL. No. No. Not seen her since the . . . since we married her.

JULIAN. It was good of you. (*The Cardinal sits in* U. R. *chair.*) I suspect she will be here soon. Butler, would you . . . go see? If she will come here? His Eminence would . . . Now do be good and go. (*Butler exits.*) He has been a great help. At times when my service has . . . perplexed me, till I grew despondent, and wondered if perhaps you'd not been mistaken in putting such a burden . . .

CARDINAL. (*Not wanting to get into it.*) Yes, yes, Julian. We have resolved it.

JULIAN. (*Crosses to* R. C. *chair.*) But then I judge it is God's doing, this . . . wrenching of my life from one light to another . . .

CARDINAL. . . . Julian . . .

JULIAN. . . . though not losing God's light, joining it with . . . my new. (*He is like a bubbling little boy.*) I can't tell you, the . . . radiance, humming, and the witchcraft, I think it must be, the ecstasy of this light, as *God's* exactly; the transport the same, the lifting, the . . . the sense of service, and the EXPANSION . . .

CARDINAL. . . . Julian . . .

JULIAN. . . . the blessed wonder of service with a renewing, not an ending joy—that joy I thought possible only through martyrdom, now, now the sunlight is no longer the hope for glare and choking in the dust and plummeting, but with cool and green and yellow dappled . . . perfumes . . .

CARDINAL. (*Sharply.*) Julian!

JULIAN. (*Little-boy smile.*) Sir.

CARDINAL. (*Evading Julian's eyes.*) We sign the papers today, Julian. It's all arranged, the grant is accomplished; through your marriage . . . your service.

JULIAN. (*Puzzlement.*) Father?

CARDINAL. (*Gestures for Julian to sit in* R. C. *chair. Barely keeping pleasure in his voice.*) And isn't it wonderful: that you have . . . found yourself such great service and such . . . exceeding happiness, too; that God's way has brought such gifts to his servant, and to his servant's servant as well.

JULIAN. (*Puzzled.*) Thank you . . . Your Eminence.

CARDINAL. (*Sadly.*) It is your wedding day, Julian!

JULIAN. (*Smiles, throws off his mood.*) Yes, it is! It's my wedding day. And a day of glory to God, that His Church has been blessed with great wealth, for the suffering of the world, conversion and the pronouncement of His Glory.

CARDINAL. (*Embarrassed, perfunctory.*) Praise God.

JULIAN. That God has seen fit to let me be His instrument in this undertaking, that God . . .

CARDINAL. Julian. (*Rises, steps* D. R. *Pause. Julian rises.*) As you have accepted what has happened . . . removed, so far removed from . . . any thought . . . accept what . . . *will* happen, *may* happen, with the same humility and . . .

JULIAN. (*Happily.*) It is my service.

CARDINAL. (*Crosses to* C. *Nods.*) Accept what may come . . . as God's will.

JULIAN. (*Crosses to the Cardinal.*) Don't . . . don't frighten me. Bless me, Father.

CARDINAL. (*Embarrassed.*) Julian, please . . .

JULIAN. (*On his knees before the Cardinal.*) Bless me?

CARDINAL. (*Reluctantly, appropriate gestures.*) In the name of the Father and of the Son and the Holy Ghost . . .

JULIAN. . . . Amen . . .

CARDINAL. . . . Amen. You *have* . . . confessed, Julian?

JULIAN. (*Blushing, but childishly pleased.*) I . . . I have, Father; I have . . . confessed, and finally, to sins more real than imagined, but . . . but they are not sins, are they, in God's name, done in God's name, Father?

73

CARDINAL. May the presence of our Lord, Jesus Christ be with you always . . .

JULIAN. . . . to . . . to shield my eyes from too much light, that I may be always worthy . . .

CARDINAL. . . . to light your way for you in the darkness . . .

JULIAN. . . . dark, darkness, Father? . . .

CARDINAL. . . . that you may be worthy of whatever sacrifice, unto death itself . . .

JULIAN. . . . in all this light! . . .

CARDINAL. . . . is asked of you; that you may accept what you do not understand . . .

JULIAN. (*A mild argument.*) But, Father . . .

CARDINAL. . . . and that the Lord may have mercy on your soul . . . as, indeed, may He have on us all . . . all our souls. (*Crosses L. to D. L.*)

JULIAN. . . . A . . . Amen?

CARDINAL. (*Nodding.*) Amen. (*Julian rises.*)

LAWYER. (*Enters U. C. with briefcase, crosses down R. steps to L. of table. The Cardinal crosses to L. of L. chair. Julian is at C.*) Well, well. Your Eminence. Julian. Well, you are indeed a fortunate man, today. What more cheering sight can there be than Frank Fearnought, clean-living, healthy farm lad, come from the heartland of the country, from the asylums—you see, I know—in search of fame, and true love—never fortune, of course.

JULIAN. . . . Please . . .

LAWYER. And see what has happened to brave and handsome Frank: he has found what he sought . . . true . . . love; *and* fortune—to his surprise, for wealth had never crossed his pure mind; and fame? . . . Ooooooh, there will be a private fame, perhaps.

CARDINAL. *Very* pretty.

LAWYER. And we are dressed in city ways, too, are we not? No longer the simple gown of the farm lad, the hems trailing in the dung; no; now we are in city clothes . . . banker's clothes.

JULIAN. These are proper clothes.

LAWYER. As you will discover, poor priestlet, poor former priestlet. Dressed differently for the sacrifice, eh?

JULIAN. (*Crosses up L. steps to platform.*) I . . . think I'll . . . look for Miss . . . for my wife.

LAWYER. Do.

74

CARDINAL. Oh, yes, Julian; please.

JULIAN. Your Eminence. (*To the Lawyer, mildly.*) We are both far too old . . . are we not . . . for all that? (*Julian exits from platform,* D. L.)

CARDINAL. (*At* L. *chair. After Julian leaves.*) Is cruelty a lesson you learned at your mother's knee? One of the songs you were taught?

LAWYER. One learns by growing, as they say. I have fine instructors behind me . . . yourself amongst them. (*A dismissing gesture.*) We have no time. (*Raises his briefcase, then throws it on a table.*) All here. (*Great cheerfulness.*) All here! The grant: all your money. (*Normal tone again.*) I must say, your Church lawyers are picky men. (*The Cardinal crosses* D. R. *to* R. *of table.*)

CARDINAL. Thorough.

LAWYER. Picky. Humorless on small matters, great wits on the major ones; ribald over the whole proposition.

CARDINAL. (*Mumbling.*) . . . hardly a subject for ribaldry . . .

LAWYER. Oh, quite a dowry, greatest marriage settlement in history, *mother* church indeed . . . things like that.

CARDINAL. (*Reaches for briefcase. Unhappily.*) Well, it's all over now . . .

LAWYER. (*Hand on the Cardinal's hand.*) Almost.

CARDINAL. (*Sits in* D. R. *chair.*) Yes.

LAWYER. (*Picks up briefcase, crosses* U. C. *to model. Puts briefcase on model, steps* C.) Cheer up; the price was high enough.

CARDINAL. Then it is . . . really true? About . . . this? (*Points at the model.*)

LAWYER. I haven't time to lie to you.

CARDINAL. Really . . . true.

LAWYER. (*Moving to the model.*) Really. Can't you accept the wonders of the world? Why not of this one, as well as the other?

CARDINAL. (*Rises, starts up* L. *steps.*) We should be . . . getting on.

LAWYER. Yes. (*Points to chapel in the model.*) Since the wedding was . . . here . . . and we are (*Indicates the room they are in.*) here . . . we have come quite a . . . dimension, have we not? (*The Lawyer crosses* D. L. *to sideboard.*)

CARDINAL. (*Abstracted.*) Yes. A distance. (*Turns, sees the Lawyer open a drawer, take out a pistol and check its cartridges.*)

75

Lawyer crosses L. of L. chair.) What . . . what are you doing? (*Moves toward the Lawyer, slowly, crossing D. L. of L. chair.*)

LAWYER. House pistol.

CARDINAL. But what are you doing?

LAWYER. (*Looking it over carefully.*) I've never shot one of these things . . . pistols. (*Then, to answer.*) I'm looking at it . . . to be sure the cartridges are there, to see that it is oiled, or whatever is done to it . . . to see how it functions.

CARDINAL. But . . .

LAWYER. (*Calmly.*) You know we may have to shoot him; you know that may be necessary.

CARDINAL. (*Sadly and softly.*) Dear God, no.

LAWYER. (*Looking at the gun.*) I suppose all you do is . . . pull. (*Looks at the Cardinal.*) If the great machinery threatens . . . to come to a halt . . . the great axis on which all turns . . . if it needs oil . . . well, we lubricate it, do we not? And if blood is the only oil handy . . . what is a little blood?

CARDINAL. (*False bravura.*) But that will not be necessary. (*Great empty quiet loss.*) Dear God, let that not be necessary.

LAWYER. Better off dead, perhaps. You know? Eh? (*He replaces gun in sideboard drawer.*)

CARDINAL. The making of a martyr? A saint?

LAWYER. Well, let's make that saint when we come to him. (*Crosses R. to R. C.*)

CARDINAL. Dear God, let that not be necessary.

LAWYER. Why not? Give me *any* person . . . a martyr, if you wish . . . a saint . . . He'll take what he gets for . . . what he wishes it to be. AH, it is what I have always wanted, he'll say, looking terror and betrayal straight in the eye. Why not: face the inevitable and call it what you have always wanted. How to come out on top, going under. (*Julian enters U. C.*) Ah! There you are. Still not with Miss Alice!

JULIAN. (*Crosses down L. steps to sideboard.*) I seem not to be with anyone.

LAWYER. (*Smile.*) Isn't that odd?

JULIAN. (*Turning away, more to himself.*) I would have thought it so.

CARDINAL. (*Crosses R. to R. of table. Hearty, but ill at ease.*) One would have thought to have it all now—corks popping, glasses splintering in the fireplace . . .

LAWYER. (*Crosses to* R. C.) When Christ told Peter—so legends tell—that he would found his church upon that rock, He must have had in mind an island in a sea of wine. How firm a foundation in the vintage years . . . (*We hear voices from without, they do, too.*)

MISS ALICE. (*Offstage.*) I don't want to go in there . . . (*Julian crosses up* L. *steps to landing. Lawyer crosses* U. *to model.*)

BUTLER. (*Offstage.*) You have to come in, now . . .

MISS ALICE. (*Offstage.*) I won't go in there. . . .

BUTLER. (*Offstage.*) Come along now; don't be a child. . . .

MISS ALICE. (*Offstage.*) I . . . won't . . . go. . . . (*Butler appears at* U. C.; *champagne bottle in one hand, pulling Miss Alice with the other. A second champagne bottle is under his arm.*)

BUTLER. Come along!

MISS ALICE. (*As she enters, sotto voce.*) I don't want to . . . (*As she sees the others see her, she stops talking, smiles, tries to save the entrance.*)

BUTLER. Lurking in the gallery, talking to the ancestral wall, but I found her.

MISS ALICE. Don't be silly; I was . . . (*Starts* L., *sees Julian, crosses* R. *and down* R. *steps. Shrugs.*)

BUTLER. (*Shrugs, too.*) Suit yourself. Champagne, everybody!

JULIAN. Ah! Good. (*Moving toward Miss Alice.*) Are you all right?

MISS ALICE. (*Moves away from him; rather impatiently.*) Yes. (*Julian crosses down* L. *steps to* C. *Butler crosses down* L. *steps to sideboard.*)

CARDINAL. But you've changed your clothes, and your wedding gown was . . .

MISS ALICE. (*Crosses to* C., *puts cloak on* R. C. *chair.*) . . . two hundred years old . . .

LAWYER. . . . fragile.

CARDINAL. Ah! (*As Julian and Miss Alice reach* C., *she moves away from him to* D. L., *leaving him alone at* C. *Something of a silence falls. The other characters are away from Julian, unless otherwise specified, they will keep a distance, surrounding him, but more than at arm's length. They will observe him, rather clinically, and while this shift of attitude must be subtle, it must also be evident. Julian will grow to knowledge of it, will aid us, though we will be aware of it before he is.*)

77

JULIAN. (*To break the silence.*) Well, shall we have the champagne?

BUTLER. (*Julian starts* L.) Stay there! (*Pause.*) I'll bring it. (*Julian steps* D.)

CARDINAL. Once, when we were in France, we toured the champagne country . . .

LAWYER. (*Crosses* D. *to* L. *of table. No interest.*) Really.

CARDINAL. Saw the . . . mechanics, so to speak, of how it was done. . . .

LAWYER. Peasants? Treading?

CARDINAL. (*Laughs.*) No, no. That is for woodcuts. (*The cork pops.*) Ah!

BUTLER. Nobody move! I'll bring it to you all. (*Starts pouring into glasses already placed to the side.*)

MISS ALICE. (*To the Lawyer.*) The ceremony. (*He does not reply, she looks at the Cardinal.*) The ceremony!

LAWYER. (*Overly sweet smile.*) Yes. (*To them all.*) The ceremony.

CARDINAL. Another? Must we officiate?

LAWYER. No need.

JULIAN. (*A little apprehensive.*) What . . . ceremony is this?

BUTLER. (*At sideboard, his back to them.*) There's never as much in a champagne bottle as I expect there to be; I never learn. Or, perhaps the glasses are larger than they seem.

LAWYER. (*Ironic.*) When the lights go on all over the world . . . the true world. The ceremony of Alice.

JULIAN. (*To Miss Alice.*) What is this about? (*She nods toward the Lawyer.*)

LAWYER. Butler? Are you poured?

BUTLER. (*Finishing, squeezing the bottle.*) Yeeeeesssss . . .

LAWYER. (*Crosses to* U. *of* R. C. *chair.*) Pass.

BUTLER. (*Starts passing the tray of glasses, crossing* R. *to Miss Alice.*) Miss Alice.

MISS ALICE. (*Strained.*) Thank you.

BUTLER. (*Starts toward Julian, changes his mind, passes him by and crosses* R. *to the Cardinal.*) Your Eminence?

CARDINAL. Ahhh.

BUTLER. (*Starts toward Julian again, changes his mind, circles* U. R. *to the Lawyer.*) Sweetheart?

LAWYER. Thank you.

BUTLER. (*Finally goes to Julian, holds the tray at arm's length, speaks, not unkindly.*) Our Brother Julian.

JULIAN. (*Shy friendliness.*) Thank you, Butler.

LAWYER. (*Steps D.*) And now . . .

BUTLER. (*Moving back L. to the sideboard with the tray.*) Hold on; I haven't got mine yet. It's over here.

JULIAN. Yes! Butler must drink with us. (*To Miss Alice.*) Don't you think so?

MISS ALICE. (*Curiously weary.*) Why not? He's family.

LAWYER. (*Moving U. L. toward the steps. Almost bumps Julian at C.*) Yes; what a large family you have.

JULIAN. I'm sorry; am . . . am I in your way?

LAWYER. (*Continues U. L. to the steps. Crosses up to U. C. Miss Alice moves D. to L. C., D. of L. chair.*) Large family, years of adding. The ceremony, children. The ceremony of Alice. (*The others have turned, are facing U. C. The Lawyer raises his glass.*) To Julian and his bride.

CARDINAL. (*At R.*) Hear, hear.

JULIAN. (*Blushing. Counters R. C.*) Oh, my goodness.

LAWYER. To Julian and his bride; to Alice's wisdom, wealth and whatever.

BUTLER. (*Quietly, seriously.*) To Alice.

MISS ALICE. To Alice. (*Brief pause, only Julian turns his head, is about to speak, but.*)

LAWYER. To their marriage. To their binding together, acceptance and worship . . . received; accepted.

BUTLER. To Alice.

LAWYER. To the marriage vow between them, which has brought joy to them both, and great benefit to the Church.

CARDINAL. Amen.

MISS ALICE. To Alice. (*Again only Julian responds to this, a half turn of the head.*)

LAWYER. To their house.

BUTLER, MISS ALICE and CARDINAL. (*Not quite together.*) To their house.

JULIAN. (*After them.*) To their house.

LAWYER. To the chapel wherein they were bound in wedlock. (*A light goes on in a room in the model. Julian makes sounds of amazement, the others are silent.*) To their quarters. (*Light goes* on *upstairs in·the model.*) To the private rooms where marriage lives.

BUTLER. To Alice.

MISS ALICE. To Alice. (*To which Julian does not respond this time.*)

LAWYER. And to this room . . . (*Another light goes on in the model.*) in which they are met, in which we are met . . . to celebrate their coming together.

BUTLER. Amen. (*Lawyer drinks.*)

LAWYER. A union whose spiritual values shall be uppermost . . .

MISS ALICE. (*Crosses* U.) That's enough. . . .

LAWYER. . . . whose carnal side shall . . .

MISS ALICE. (*Turns* D.) That's enough!

JULIAN. May . . . May I? (*He crosses up* R. *steps to top of platform,* R. *It is important that he stay facing the model, not Miss Alice. Butler, who is behind him, may look at him, the Cardinal will look to the floor.*) May I . . . propose. To the wonders . . . which may befall a man . . . least where he is looking, least that he would have thought; to the clear plan of that which we call chance, to what we see as accident till our humility returns to us when we are faced with the mysteries. To all that which we really want, until our guile and pride . . .

CARDINAL. (*Still looking at the floor.*) . . . Julian . . .

JULIAN. . . . betray us? (*Looks at the Cardinal, pauses, goes on, smiling sweetly.*) My gratitude . . . my wonder . . . and my love.

LAWYER. (*Pause.*) Amen?

JULIAN. Amen. (*All finish drinks.*)

LAWYER. (*Abruptly turning, crosses down* L. *steps, puts glass on sideboard, crosses* U. L. C. *Miss Alice crosses to Butler, gives him glass.*) Then, if we're packed, let us go.

BUTLER. (*Not moving.*) Dust covers.

JULIAN. (*Still smiling, crosses down* R. *steps.*) Go?

CARDINAL. (*To delay. Crosses* U. L. *towards sideboard. Meets Lawyer.*) Well. This champagne glass seems smaller than one would have guessed; it has emptied itself . . . on one toast!

LAWYER. I recall. Suddenly I recall it. When we were children. (*Quite fascinated with what he is saying.*) When we were children and we would gather in the dark, two of us . . . any two . . . on a swing, side porch, or by the ocean, sitting backed against a boulder, and we would explore . . . those most private parts, of one another, any two of us . . . (*Shrugs.*) boy, girl, how—when we did it—we would talk of other things . . . of our schoolwork, or where we would travel in the summer. How, as our shaking hands passed under skirts or undid buttons, sliding, how we would, both of us, talk of other things, whispering, our voices shaking as our just barely moving hands. (*Laughs, points to the Cardinal.*) Like you! Chattering there on the model! Your mind on us and what is happening. Oh, the subterfuges. (*The Cardinal crosses to sideboard, gives glass to Butler.*)

MISS ALICE. I am packed.

JULIAN. (*Still off by himself, at* R. C.) Packed? . . . Miss Alice?

MISS ALICE. (*Crosses* U. *To the Lawyer, cold.*) May we leave soon?

JULIAN. (*Crossing* L. *to Lawyer and Miss Alice.*) Miss . . . Alice?

MISS ALICE. May we?

LAWYER. (*Pause.*) Fairly.

JULIAN. (*Sharp.*) Miss Alice!

MISS ALICE. (*Crosses* R. *to* R. C. *chair, picks up cloak. Crosses* D. R., *ignoring Julian, flat tone, a recitation.*) I'm very happy for you, Julian, you've done well.

JULIAN. (*Backing away from everyone a little.*) What is . . . going on . . . here? (*To Miss Alice.*) Tell me! (*Butler takes sheet from back of* L. *chair, puts on* L. *newel post.*)

MISS ALICE. (*As if she is not interested.*) I am packed. We are going. (*She puts on cloak.*)

JULIAN. (*Sudden understanding.*) Ah! (*Points to himself.*) *We* are going. But where? You . . . didn't tell me we . . . we were . . .

MISS ALICE. (*To the Lawyer, moving away.*) Tell him.

JULIAN. . . . going somewhere. . . .

MISS ALICE. (*Quite furious.*) Tell him!

LAWYER. (*About to make a speech. Steps to* D. L. C., *gestures for Julian to sit in* L. *chair.*) Brother Julian . . .

JULIAN. (*Strained.*) I am no longer Brother.

LAWYER. (*Oily.*) Oh, are we not all brothers?

JULIAN. (*To Miss Alice, with a halfhearted gesture.*) Come stand by me.

MISS ALICE. (*Surprisingly little-girl fright.*) No! (*Julian crosses* L. *to* L. *chair.*)

LAWYER. Now. Julian.

CARDINAL. (*Turns* D., *at* D. L.) Order yourself, Julian.

JULIAN. (*Sits in* L. *chair. To the Cardinal.*) Sir? (*Miss Alice faces* D. R., *the Cardinal faces* D. L.; *Butler faces* U.)

LAWYER. (*Sarcasm is gone, all is gone, save fact.*) Dear Julian; we all serve, do we not? Each of us his own priesthood; publicly, some, others . . . within only; but we all do—what's-his-name's special trumpet, or clear lonely bell. Predestination, fate, the will of God, accident . . . All swirled up in it, no matter what the name. And being man, we have invented choice, and have, indeed, gone further, and have catalogued the underpinnings of choice. But we do not know. Anything. End prologue.

MISS ALICE. Tell him.

LAWYER. No matter. We are leaving you now, Julian; agents, every one of us—going. We are leaving you . . . to your accomplishments: your marriage, your wife, your . . . special priesthood.

JULIAN. (*Apprehension and great suspicion.*) I . . . don't know what you're talking about.

LAWYER. (*Unperturbed. The Cardinal, Miss Alice and Butler turn in to Julian.*) What is so amazing is the . . . coming together . . . of disparates . . . left-fielding, out of the most unlikely. Who would have thought, Julian? Who would have thought? You have brought us to the end of our service here. (*He crosses* R. *to* L. *of table.*) We go on; you stay.

BUTLER. May I begin to cover?

MISS ALICE. (*Crosses to* C.) Not yet. (*Kindly.*) Do you understand, Julian?

JULIAN. (*Barely in control.*) Of course not!

MISS ALICE. Julian, I have tried to be . . . her. No; I have tried to be . . . what I thought she might, what might make you happy, what you might use, as a . . . what?

BUTLER. Play God; go on.

MISS ALICE. We must . . . represent, draw pictures, reduce or enlarge to . . . to what we can understand.

JULIAN. (*Sad, mild.*) But I have fought against it . . . all my life. When they said, "Bring the wonders down to me, closer; I

82

cannot see them, touch; nor can I believe." I have fought against it . . . all my life.

BUTLER. (*To Miss Alice, softly.*) You see? No good.

MISS ALICE. (*Shrugs.*) I have done what I can with it.

JULIAN. All my life. In and out of . . . confinement, fought against the symbol.

MISS ALICE. Then you should be happy now.

CARDINAL. Julian, it has been your desire always to serve; your sense of mission . . .

LAWYER. We are surrogates; our task is done now.

MISS ALICE. Stay with her.

JULIAN. (*Rises. Horror behind it, disbelieving.*) Stay . . . with . . . her?

MISS ALICE. Stay with her. Accept it.

LAWYER. (*Crosses u. to u. R. of L. chair, towards model.*) Her rooms are lighted. It is warm, there is enough.

MISS ALICE. Be content with it. Stay with her.

JULIAN. (*Refusing to accept what he is hearing.*) Miss Alice . . . I have married you.

MISS ALICE. (*Kind, still.*) No, Julian; you have married her . . . through me.

JULIAN. (*Pointing to the model.*) There is nothing there! We are here! There is no one there!

LAWYER. (*Steps D.*) She is there . . . we believe.

JULIAN. (*To Miss Alice. He starts towards her.*) I have been with you!

MISS ALICE. (*Not explaining, sort of dreamy. She backs R. to D. R. C.*) You have felt her warmth through me, touched her lips through my lips, held hands, through mine, my breasts, hers, lain on her bed, through mine, wrapped yourself in her wings, your hands on the small of her back, your mouth on her hair, the voice in your ear, hers not mine, all hers; her. You are hers. (*Julian turns L.*)

CARDINAL. Accept.

BUTLER. Accept.

LAWYER. Accept.

JULIAN. (*Turns to Miss Alice.*) THERE IS NO ONE THERE!

MISS ALICE. She is there.

JULIAN. (*Rushes u. c. to the model, shouts at it.*) THERE IS

83

NOTHING THERE! (*Turns to them all.*) THERE IS NOTHING THERE!

CARDINAL. (*Softly.*) Accept it, Julian.

JULIAN. (*Crosses* D. L. *to the Cardinal. All the power he has.*) ACCEPT IT!

LAWYER. (*Crosses* R. *to* L. *of table. Quietly.*) All legal, all accomplished, all satisfied, that which we believe.

JULIAN. ACCEPT!

BUTLER. (*At* U. L. *of* L. *chair.*) . . . that which is done, and may not be revoked.

CARDINAL. (*With some difficulty.*) . . . yes.

JULIAN. WHAT AM I TO ACCEPT!

LAWYER. An act of faith.

JULIAN. (*Slow, incredulous.*) An . . . act . . . of . . . faith!

LAWYER. (*Snaps his fingers at the Cardinal.*) Buddy?

CARDINAL. Uh . . . yes, Julian, an . . . act of faith, indeed. It is . . . believed.

LAWYER. (*Deadly serious, but with a small smile.*) Yes, it is . . . believed. It is what we believe, therefore what we know. Is that not right? Faith is knowledge?

CARDINAL. An act of faith, Julian, however we must . . .

JULIAN. (*Horror.*) FAITH!?

CARDINAL. . . . in God's will . . .

JULIAN. GOD'S! WILL!

CARDINAL. (*As if his ears are hurting, sort of mumbling.*) Yes, Julian, you see, we must accept, and . . . be glad, yes, be glad . . . our ecstasy.

JULIAN. (*Backing off a little to* C., *shaking his head.*) I have not come this distance . . .

CARDINAL. *Moving toward him a little.*) Julian . . .

JULIAN. Stay back! I have not come this long way . . . have not —in all sweet obedience—walked in these . . . (*Realizes he is differently dressed.*) those robes . . . to be MOCKED.

LAWYER. Accept it, Julian.

JULIAN. I have not come this long *way!*

BUTLER. Yes; oh, yes. (*Lawyer starts slowly* U. L. *to* L. *steps and up to landing. Butler starts slowly* U. R. *to* R. *steps and up to landing.*)

JULIAN. I HAVE NOT!

84

MISS ALICE. (*Kindly.*) Julian . . . dear Julian; accept. (*She starts up* R. *steps to* C. *of* U. *platform.*)

JULIAN. (*At table,* R. C. *Turns toward her, supplicating.*) I have not worn and given up for . . . for mockery; I have not stretched out the path of my life before me, to walk on straight, to be . . .

MISS ALICE. Accept.

JULIAN. I have not fought the nightmares—and the waking demons, yes—and the years of despair, those, too . . . (*Crosses* U. C. *to model.*) I have not accepted *half,* for *nothing.*

CARDINAL. For everything.

MISS ALICE. Dear Julian; accept. Allow us all to rest.

JULIAN. (*A child's terror of being alone.*) NO! (*Crosses to* R. C. *chair, sits.*)

MISS ALICE. (*Still kind.*) You must.

BUTLER. No choice.

JULIAN. I have . . . have . . . given up everything to gain everything, for the sake of my faith and my peace; I have allowed and followed, and sworn and cherished, but I have *not,* have *not* . . .

MISS ALICE. Be with her. Please.

JULIAN. For hallucination? I HAVE DONE WITH HALLUCINATION.

MISS ALICE. Then have done with forgery, Julian; accept what's real. I am the . . . illusion.

JULIAN. (*Retreating.*) No . . . no no no, oh no.

LAWYER. (*Quietly.*) All legal, all accomplished, all satisfied, that which we believe.

MISS ALICE. All done.

JULIAN. (*Quite frightened.*) I . . . choose . . . *not.*

CARDINAL. There is no choice here, Julian. . . .

LAWYER. No choice at all. (*Butler crosses* D. *to* R. *of* R. C. *chair. Lawyer crosses* D. *to* C. *Miss Alice crosses* D. *to* R. *of table.*)

MISS ALICE. (*Hands apart.*) All done. (*Julian rises, begins backing toward the model, the Lawyer begins crossing to the sideboard wherein he has put the gun.*)

BUTLER. (*Quietly.*) I *must* cover now; the cars are waiting.

JULIAN. No . . . no . . . I WILL NOT ACCEPT THIS.

LAWYER. (*Snaps for the Cardinal again.*) Buddy . . .

CARDINAL. We . . . (*Harder tone.*) I order you.

LAWYER. (*Smile.*) There. Now will you accept?

85

JULIAN. I . . . cannot be so mistaken, to have . . . I cannot have so misunderstood my life; I cannot have . . . was I sane then? Those *years*? My time in the *asylum*? WAS THAT WHEN I WAS RATIONAL? THEN?

CARDINAL. Julian . . .

LAWYER. (*Taking the gun from the drawer, checking it, to the Cardinal.*) Don't you teach your people anything? Do you let them improvise? *Make* their Gods? *Make* them as they *see* them?

JULIAN. (*Rage in the terror.*) I HAVE ACCEPTED GOD.

LAWYER. (*Crosses to L. of R. chair. Turns to Julian, gun in hand.*) Then accept his works. Resign yourself to the mysteries . . .

MISS ALICE. . . . to greater wisdom.

LAWYER. Take it! Accept what you're given.

MISS ALICE. Your priesthood, Julian—full, at last. Stay with her. Accept your service.

JULIAN. I . . . cannot . . . accept . . . this.

LAWYER. (*Aims.*) Very well, then.

JULIAN. I have not come this . . . given up so much for . . .

BUTLER. Accept it, Julian.

MISS ALICE. Stay with her.

JULIAN. No, no, I will . . . I will go *back!* I will . . . go *back* to it. (*Crosses D. L.*) To . . . to . . . I will go back to the asylum.

LAWYER. Last chance.

MISS ALICE. Accept it, Julian.

JULIAN. (*Crosses u. to foot of L. steps.*) To . . . my asylum. MY! ASYLUM! My . . . my refuge . . . in the world, from all the demons waking, my . . . REFUGE!

LAWYER. Very well then. (*Shoots. Then silence. Julian does not cry out, but clutches his belly, stumbles forward a few steps, sinks to the floor in front of the model. He crawls to R. of L. chair.*)

MISS ALICE. (*Softly, with compassion.*) Oh, Julian. (*To the Lawyer, calm.*) He would have stayed.

LAWYER. (*To Miss Alice, shrugging. Crosses to sideboard, puts gun away.*) It was an accident.

JULIAN. Fa . . . ther?

MISS ALICE. Poor Julian. (*To the Lawyer.*) You did not have to do that; I could have made him stay.

LAWYER. Perhaps. But what does it matter . . . one man . . . in the face of so much.

86

JULIAN. Fa . . . ther?

BUTLER. (*Going to Julian.*) Let me look.

MISS ALICE. (*Starting to go to him.*) Oh, poor JULIAN . . .

LAWYER. (*Stopping her.*) Stay where you are. (*Butler goes to Julian while the others keep their places. Butler bends over him, maybe pulling his head back.*)

BUTLER. Do you want a doctor for him?

LAWYER. (*After a tiny pause.*) Why?

BUTLER. (*Straightening up.*) Because . . .

LAWYER. Yes?

BUTLER. (*Quite matter-of-fact.*) Because he will bleed to death without attention?

JULIAN. (*To the Cardinal.*) Help . . . me? (*In answer, the Cardinal looks back to the Lawyer, asking a question with his silence.*)

LAWYER. (*After a pause.*) No doctor.

BUTLER. (*Moving away.*) No doctor.

MISS ALICE. (*To the Lawyer, great sadness.*) No?

LAWYER. (*Some compassion.*) No.

JULIAN. Father!

CARDINAL. (*Anguished.*) Please, Julian.

JULIAN. (*Anger through the pain.*) In the sight of God? You dare?

LAWYER. Or in the sight of man. He dares. (*He crosses u. to model, picks up briefcase and circles Julian, crossing D. L. to the Cardinal.*)

JULIAN. (*Again.*) You dare!? (*Butler goes to cover something.*)

LAWYER. (*Putting briefcase down between himself and the Cardinal.*) There it is, all of it. All legal now, the total grant: two billion, kid, twenty years of grace for no work at all; no labor . . . at least not yours. There . . . take it.

CARDINAL. We do not . . . fetch and carry. And have not acquiesced . . . (*Indicates briefcase.*) For this.

JULIAN. (*Weak again.*) Father?

LAWYER. Not God's errand boy?

CARDINAL. God's; not yours.

LAWYER. *Who* are the Gods?

JULIAN. (*Pain.*) God in heaven!

MISS ALICE. Poor Julian! (*Goes to him, kneels, they create something of a Pietà.*) Rest back; lean on me.

LAWYER. (*Withdrawing his offer of the briefcase.*) Perhaps your *new* secretary can pick it up. You *will* go on, won't you—red gown and amethyst, until the pelvic cancer comes, or the coronary blacks it out, all of it? The good with it, and the evil? (*Indicates Julian.*) Even this? In the final mercy? (*The Cardinal looks straight ahead of him for a moment, hesitates, then crosses up L. steps and out U. C. doors, looking neither left nor right.*)

BUTLER. (*Calling after him, halfhearted and intentionally too late.*) Any of the cars will do . . . (*Trailing off.*) . . . as they're all hired.

JULIAN. Who . . . who left? Who!

MISS ALICE. (*Comforting him.*) You're shivering, Julian . . . so.

JULIAN. (*Almost a laugh.*) Am I?

LAWYER. (*Still looking after the departed Cardinal.*) Once, when I was at school—our departed reminds me—once, when I was at school, I was writing poetry—well, no, poems, which were published in the literary magazine. And each issue a teacher from the English Department would criticize the work in the school newspaper a week or two hence.

MISS ALICE. (*To Julian.*) A blanket?

JULIAN. No. Hold close. (*Butler moves chairs around R. table, covering them with sheets.*)

LAWYER. And one teacher, who was a wag and was, as well, a former student, wrote of one of my poems—a sonnet, as I recall—that it had all the grace of a walking crow.

MISS ALICE. (*Ibid.*) I don't want to hurt.

JULIAN. Closer . . . please. Warmth.

LAWYER. I was green in those years, and, besides, I could not recall how crows walked.

MISS ALICE. (*Ibid.*) How like a little boy you are.

JULIAN. I'm lonely.

LAWYER. Could not recall that I had ever *seen* a crow . . . walking.

MISS ALICE. Is being afraid always the same—no matter the circumstances, the age?

JULIAN. It is the attic room, always; the closet. Hold close.

LAWYER. (*Fully aware of the counterpoint by now, aiding it.*) And so I went to see him—the wag—about the walking crow . . . the poem, actually.

BUTLER. (*Putting a cover on something.*) Crows don't walk much . . .

JULIAN. . . . and it is very dark; always. And no one will come . . . for the longest time.

MISS ALICE. Yes.

LAWYER. Yes; that is what he said—sitting with his back against all the books, "Crows don't walk much . . . if they can help it . . . if they can fly."

JULIAN. No. No one will come.

BUTLER. (*Snapping open a cover.*) I could have told you that; surprised you didn't know it. Crows walk around a lot only when they're sick.

LAWYER. "Santayanian finesse."

JULIAN. No one will come . . . for the longest time; if ever.

MISS ALICE. (*Agreeing.*) No.

LAWYER. That was the particular thing: "Santayanian finesse." He said that had . . . all the grace of a walking crow.

BUTLER. (*Rubbing something for dust.*) Bright man.

LAWYER. (*To Butler.*) I don't know; he stayed on some years after I left—after our walking bird and I left—then went on to some other school. . . . (*To Miss Alice, immediately.*) Are you ready to go?

MISS ALICE. (*Looking up; sad irony.*) Am I ready to go on with it, do you mean? To move to the city now before the train trip south? The private car? The house on the ocean, the . . . same mysteries, the evasions, the perfect plotting? The removed residence, the Rolls twice weekly into the shopping strip . . . all of it?

LAWYER. Yes. All of it.

MISS ALICE. (*Looks to Julian, considers a moment.*) Are you warm now?

JULIAN. Yes . . . and cold.

MISS ALICE. (*Looks up to the Lawyer, smiles faintly.*) No.

LAWYER. Then get up and come along.

MISS ALICE. (*To the Lawyer.*) And all the rest of it?

LAWYER. Yes.

MISS ALICE. The years of it . . . to go on? For how long?

LAWYER. Until we are replaced.

MISS ALICE. (*With a tiny, tinkling laugh.*) Oh God.

LAWYER. Or until everything is desert (*Shrugs.*) . . . on the chance that it runs out before *we* do.

BUTLER. (*Examining the phrenological head.*) I have never even examined phrenology.

LAWYER. But more likely till we are replaced.

JULIAN. (*With a sort of quiet wonder.*) I am cold at the core . . . where it burns most.

MISS ALICE. (*Sad truth.*) Yes. (*Then to the Lawyer.*) Yes.

LAWYER. (*Almost affectionately.*) So, come now; gather yourself.

MISS ALICE. (*Restrained pleading.*) But, he is still . . . ill . . .

JULIAN. (*To Miss Alice, probably, but not at her.*) You wish to go away now?

MISS ALICE. (*To the Lawyer.*) You see how he takes to me? You see how it *is* natural? Poor Julian.

LAWYER. Let's go.

MISS ALICE. (*To Julian.*) I *must* go away from you now; it is not that I wish to. (*To Butler.*) Butler, I have left my wig, it is upstairs . . .

BUTLER. (*Rather testy.*) I'm sorry, I'm covering, I'm busy.

LAWYER. (*Turning to go.*) Let me; it's such a pretty wig, becomes you so. And there are one or two other things I'd like to check.

MISS ALICE. (*Sad smile.*) The pillowcases? Put your ear against them? To eavesdrop? Or the sheets? To see if they're still writhing? (*The Lawyer almost says something, thinks better of it, crosses up* L. *steps and out* D. L. *arch.*) Poor Julian.

BUTLER. Then we all are to be together.

MISS ALICE. (*Small laugh.*) Oh God, you heard him: forever.

BUTLER. I like it where it's warm. (*Crosses to* L. *of* C. *table, picks up Julian's glass.*)

MISS ALICE. I dreaded once, when I was in my teens, that I would grow old, look back, over the precipice, and discover that I had not lived my life. (*Short abrupt laugh.*) Oh Lord!

JULIAN. (*Now a semi-coma, almost sweet.*) How long wilt thou forget me, O Lord? Forever?

BUTLER. (*Crosses* L. *to sideboard.*) We live *something.*

MISS ALICE. Yes.

JULIAN. How long wilt thou hide thy face from me?

BUTLER. (*To Julian.*) Psalm Thirteen.

MISS ALICE. (*To Julian.*) Yes?

JULIAN. Yes.

BUTLER. How long shall my enemy be exalted over me?

JULIAN. Yes.

MISS ALICE. Not long.

BUTLER. (*Looking at a cover.*) Consider and hear me, O Lord, my God.

JULIAN. What does it mean if the pain . . . ebbs?

BUTLER. (*Crosses to U. of L. chair. Considered, kindly.*) It means the agony is less.

MISS ALICE. Yes.

JULIAN. (*Rueful laugh.*) Consciousness, then, is pain. (*Looks up at Miss Alice.*) All disappointments, all treacheries. (*Ironic laugh.*) Oh, God.

BUTLER. Why are we taking separate cars, then?

MISS ALICE. Well, I might ride rubbing hips on either side with a different lover, bouncing along, but . . . Alice, Miss Alice would not. (*Pause.*) Would I? I would not do that. She.

BUTLER. I love you . . . not her. Or . . . quite differently.

MISS ALICE. Shhhh . . .

BUTLER. (*Moves L. chair to L., facing sideboard.*) For ages, I look at the sheets, listen to the pillowcases, when they're brought down, sidle into the laundry room . . .

MISS ALICE. Don't. (*Julian makes a sound of great pain.*) Oh! . . . Oh! . . .

JULIAN. (*Commenting on the pain.*) Dear . . . God . . . in . . . heaven . . .

MISS ALICE. Calm; be calm now.

BUTLER. (*Wistful.*) But you pass through everyone, everything . . . touching just briefly, lightly, passing. (*He covers L. chair.*)

MISS ALICE. My poor Julian. (*To the model.*) Receive him? Take him in?

JULIAN. (*A little boy, scared.*) Who are you talking to?

MISS ALICE. (*Breathing it.*) Alice . . .

JULIAN. Alice? Ah.

BUTLER. Will we be coming back . . . when the weather changes?

MISS ALICE. (*Triste.*) Probably.

JULIAN. (*Confirming the previous exchange.*) Alice?

MISS ALICE. Yes.

JULIAN. Ah.

BUTLER. (*Understanding what he has been told.*) Ah. (*The Lawyer enters* L. *with Miss Alice's wig. Crosses down* L. *steps, stops at bottom. Butler crosses up* L. *steps to landing and covers globe.*)

LAWYER. Bed stripped, mothballs lying on it like hailstones; no sound, movement, nothing. (*Puts the wig on the phrenological head. Then crosses to* L. *of Julian with head, puts it down at Julian's feet.*) Do you want company, Julian? Do you want a friend? (*To Miss Alice.*) Looks nice there. Leave it; we'll get you another. Are you ready to go? (*Steps* U. *to Miss Alice. Butler crosses down* L. *steps to bottom.*)

MISS ALICE. (*Weary.*) You want me to go now?

LAWYER. (*Correcting her.*) Come.

MISS ALICE. Yes. (*Begins to disengage herself.*) Butler, come help me; we can't leave Julian just . . .

BUTLER. Yes. (*Moves to help her.*)

JULIAN. (*As they take him by the arm.*) Don't do that!

MISS ALICE. Julian, we must move you . . .

JULIAN. Don't.

LAWYER. (*Without emotion.*) Leave him where he is.

JULIAN. Leave me . . . be. (*He slides along the floor, backing up against the model.*) Leave me . . . where I am.

LAWYER. Good pose: leave him there.

BUTLER. (*Getting a chair cushion.*) Cushion.

JULIAN. All . . . hurts.

BUTLER. (*Putting the cushion behind him.*) Easy . . . .

JULIAN. ALL HURTS!!

MISS ALICE. (*Coming to him.*) Oh, my poor Julian . . .

JULIAN. (*Surprisingly strong, angry.*) LEAVE ME! (*Miss Alice considers a moment, turns, leaves, crossing up* R. *stairs and out* U. C. *doors to* R.)

LAWYER. (*Walks over to Julian, regards him, almost casually.*) Goodbye.

JULIAN. (*Softly, but a malediction.*) Instrument!

LAWYER. (*Turns on his heel, crosses up* R. *stairs to* U. C. *doors, saying as he goes.*) Butler? (*Exits* R.)

BUTLER. (*At* L. *chair. As Lawyer goes, abstracted.*) Yes . . . dear.

JULIAN. (*Half laughed, pained incredulity.*) Good . . . bye!

92

BUTLER. (*Looks about the room.*) All in order, I think.

JULIAN. (*Wistful.*) Help me?

BUTLER. My work done.

JULIAN. No? (*Butler regards Julian for a moment, then walks over, kneels, kisses Julian on the forehead, not a quick kiss.*)

BUTLER. Goodbye, dear Julian. (*As Butler exits, crossing up R. stairs to U. C., he closes the doors behind him.*)

JULIAN. (*Alone, for a moment, then, whispered.*) Goodbye, dear Julian. (*Pause.*) Exit . . . all. (*Softly.*) Help me . . . come back, help me. (*Pause.*) HELP ME! (*Pause.*) No . . . no help. Kiss. A kiss goodbye, from . . . whom? . . . Oh. From, from one . . . an . . . arms: around me; warming. COME BACK AND HELP ME. (*Pause.*) If only to stay *with* me, while it . . . *if* . . . while it happens. For . . . you, you would not have left me if it . . . were not . . . would you? No. (*Calling to them.*) I HAVE NEVER DREAMED OF IT. NEVER . . . IMAGINED . . . (*To himself again.*) what it would be like. (*As if they were near the door.*) I died once, when I was little . . . almost, running, fell past jagged iron, noticed . . . only when I . . . tried to get up, that my leg, left, was torn . . . the whole thigh and calf . . . down. Such . . . *searing* . . . pain? Sweet smell of blood, screaming at the sight of it, so *far* . . . away from the house, and in the field, all hot . . . and yellow, white in the sun. COME BACK TO ME. Sunday, and my parents off . . . somewhere, only my grandfather, and he . . . OFF: SOMEWHERE: mousing with the dog. All the way down . . . bone, flesh, meat, moving. Help me, Grandfather! "Ere I die, ere life ebbs." (*Laughs softly.*) Oh, Christ. (*Little boy.*) Grandfather? Mousing? Come to me: Julian bleeds, leg torn, from short pants to shoe, bone, meat open to the sun; come to him. (*Looks at the model, above and behind him.*) Ahhhh. Will no one come? (*Looks at the ceiling.*) High; high walls . . . summit. (*Eyes on his leg.*) Belly . . . not leg. Come, grandfather! Not leg, belly! Double-button. Pinpoint, searing . . . pain? "If you . . . if you die." Are you sleeping, not mousing? Sleeping on the sunporch? Hammocking? Yes. "If I die before *you* wake, will the Lord deign *your* soul take?" Grandfather? (*Cry of pain, then.*) Oh . . . GOD! "I come to thee, in agony." (*Cry to the void.*) HELP . . . ME! (*Pause.*) No help. Stitch it up like a wineskin! Hold the wine in. Stitch it up. (*Sweet reminiscence.*) And every day, put him in the sun, quarter

93

over, for the whole stitched leg . . . to bake, in the healing sun. Green? Yes, a little, but that's the medicine. And keep him out of the fields, chuckle, chuckle. And every day, swinging in the sun, baking; good. Aching all the while, but good. The cat comes, sniffs it, won't stay. Finally . . . stays; lies in the bend, doubling it, purring, breathing, soaking in the sun, as the leg throbs, aches, heals. "How will I know thee, O Lord, when I am in thy sight? How will I know thee?" By my *faith*. Ah, I see. (*Furious, shouting at the roof.*) BY FAITH? THE FAITH I HAVE SHOWN THEE? BENT MYSELF? What may we avoid! Not birth! Growing up? Yes. Maturing? Oh, *God!* Growing old, and? . . . yes, growing old; but not the last; merely when. (*Sweet singsong.*) But to live again, be born once more, sure in the sight of . . . (*Shouts again.*) THERE IS NO ONE! (*Turns his head toward the closed doors, sadly.*) Unless you are listening there. Unless you have left me, tiptoed off some, stood whispering, smothered giggles, and . . . silently returned, your ears pressed against, or . . . or one eye into the crack so that the air smarts it sifting through. HAVE YOU COME BACK? HAVE YOU NOT LEFT ME? (*Pause.*) No. No one. Out in the night . . . nothing. Night? No; what then? IS IT NIGHT . . . OR DAY? (*Great weariness.*) Or does it matter? No. How long wilt thou forget me, O Lord? Forever? How long wilt thou hide thy face from me? How long shall my enemy . . . I . . . can . . . barely . . . feel. Which is a sign. A change, at any rate. (*To the rooftops again.*) I DO NOT UNDERSTAND, O LORD, MY GOD, WHAT THOU WILT HAVE OF ME! (*More conversational.*) I have never dreamed of it, never imagined what it would be like. I have—oh, yes—dwelt (*Laughs at the word.*) . . . dwelt . . . on the *fact* of it, the . . . principle, but I have not imagined dying. Death . . . yes. Not being, but not the act of . . . dying? ALICE!? (*Laughs softly.*) Oh, Alice, why hast *thou* forsaken me? (*Leans his head back to see the model.*) Hast thou? Alice? *Hast* thou forsaken me . . . with . . . all the others? (*Laughs again.*) Come bring me my slippers and my pipe, and push the dog into the room. Bring me my slippers, the sacramental wine, (*Little boy.*) my cookie? (*Usual again.*) . . . come bring me my ease, come sit with me . . . and watch me as I die. Alice? ALICE!? (*To himself.*) There is nothing; there is no one. (*Wheedling a little.*) Come talk to me; come sit by my right hand . . . on the one hand . . . come sit with me and hold my . . . what? Then come and talk; tell me how it goes, Alice. (*Laughs.*) "Raise high the roofbeam, for the bridegroom comes." Oh, what a priesthood is this! Oh, what a range of duties, and such parishioners, and such a chapel for my praise. (*Turns some, leans toward the model, where the chapel light shines.*) Oh, what a priesthood, see my chapel, how it . . . (*Suddenly the light in the chapel in the model goes out. Julian starts, makes a sound of surprise and fear.*) Alice? . . . God? SOMEONE? Come to Julian as he . . . ebbs. (*We begin to hear it now, faintly at first, slowly growing, so faintly at first it is subliminal: the heartbeat . . . thump thump . . . thump thump . . . And the breathing . . . the intake taking one thump-thump, the exhaling the next. Julian neither senses nor hears it yet, however.*) Come, comfort him, warm him. He has not been a willful man . . . Oh, willful in his . . . cry to serve, but gentle, would not cause pain, but bear it, would bear it . . . has, even. Not much, I suppose. One man's share is not . . . another's burden. (*Notices the wig on the phrenological head, crawls a bit toward it; half kneels in front of it.*) Thou art my bride? Thou? For thee have I done my life? Grown to love, entered in, bent . . . accepted? For thee? Is that the . . . awful humor? Art thou the true arms, when the warm flesh I touched . . . rested against, was . . . nothing? And she . . . was not real? Is thy stare the true look? Unblinking, outward, through, to some horizon? And her eyes . . . warm, accepting, were they . . . not real? Art thou my bride? (*To the ceiling again.*) Ah God! Is that the humor? THE ABSTRACT? . . . REAL? THE REST? . . . FALSE? (*To himself, with terrible irony.*) It is what I have wanted, have insisted on. Have nagged . . . for. (*Looking about the room, raging.*) IS THIS MY PRIESTHOOD, THEN? THIS WORLD? THEN COME AND SHOW THYSELF! BRIDE? GOD? (*Silence; we hear the heartbeats and the breathing some.*) SHOW THYSELF! I DEMAND THEE! (*Julian crawls back toward the model, faces it, back to the audience, addresses it.*) SHOW THYSELF! FOR THEE I HAVE GAMBLED . . . MY SOUL? I DEMAND THY PRESENCE. ALICE! (*The sounds become louder now, as, in the model, the light fades in the bedroom, begins to move across an upper story. Julian's reaction is a muffled cry.*) AGHHH! (*On his hands and knees he backs off a little from the model, still staring at it.*)

You . . . thou . . . art . . . coming to me? (*Frightened and angry.*) ABSTRACTION? . . . ABSTRACTION! . . . (*Sad, defeated.*) Art coming to me. (*A shivered prayer, quick.*) How long wilt thou forget me, O Lord? Forever? How long wilt thou hide thy face from me? . . . Consider and hear me, O Lord, my God. (*Shouted now.*) CONSIDER AND HEAR ME, O LORD, MY GOD. LIGHTEN MY EYES LEST I SLEEP THE SLEEP OF DEATH. (*The lights keep moving, the sounds become louder.*) BUT I HAVE TRUSTED IN THY MERCY, O LORD. HOW LONG WILT THOU FORGET ME? (*Softly, whining.*) How long wilt thou hide thy face from me? COME, BRIDE! COME, GOD! COME! (*The breathing and heartbeats are much, much louder now. The lights descend a stairway in the model. Julian turns, backs against the model, his arms way to the side of him.*) Alice? (*Fear and trembling.*) Alice? ALICE? MY GOD, WHY HAST THOU FORSAKEN ME? (*A great shadow, or darkening, fills the stage, it is the shadow of a great presence filling the room. The area on Julian and around him stays in some light, but, for the rest, it is as if ink were moving through paper toward a focal point. The sounds become enormous. Julian is aware of the presence in the room, "sees" it, in the sense that his eyes, his head move to all areas of the room, noticing his engulfment. He almost-whispers loudly.*) The bridegroom waits for thee, my Alice . . . is thine. O Lord, my God, I have awaited thee, have served thee in thy . . . ALICE? (*His arms are wide, should resemble a crucifixion. With his hands on the model, he will raise his body some, backed full up against it.*) ALICE? . . . GOD? (*The sounds are deafening. Julian smiles faintly.*) I accept thee, Alice, for thou art come to me. God, Alice . . . I accept thy will. (*Sounds continue. Julian dies, head bows, body relaxes some, arms stay wide in the crucifixion. Sounds continue thusly: thrice after the death . . . thump thump thump thump thump thump. Absolute silence for two beats. The lights on Julian fade slowly to black. Only then, when all is black, does the curtain slowly fall.*)

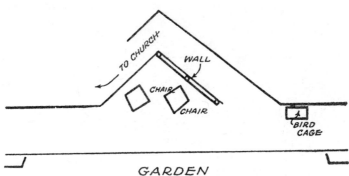

GARDEN
ACT I -- SCENE 1

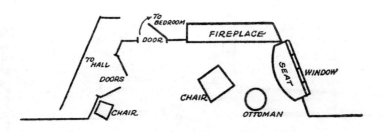

SITTING ROOM

SCENE DESIGNS
ACT I -- SCENE 3
AND ACT II -- SCENE 3

"TINY ALICE"

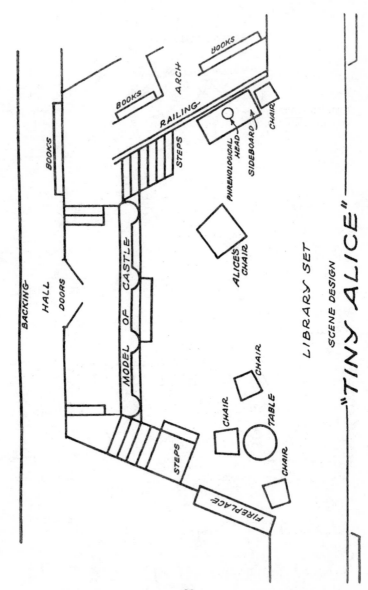

LIBRARY SET

SCENE DESIGN

"TINY ALICE"

PROPERTY PLOT

Act 1, Scene 1—Garden

Preset:

2 garden chairs
Walking stick (Lawyer)
Fan (Cardinal)
Birdcage
Fountain

Personal:

Cigarette case ⎫
Lighter   ⎬ (Lawyer)
Notebook, pencil ⎭
Ring, on 3rd finger R. hand ⎫
Handkerchief   ⎬ (Cardinal)

Act 1, Scene 2—Library

Port glasses   ⎫
Liqueur glasses   ⎪
Champagne glasses ⎬ in sideboard
Scotch bottle   ⎪
Shot glasses   ⎪
Bottle of port   ⎭
Cigarette box—on table
Silver salver—sideboard
4 chairs
1 round table
1 sideboard
1 globe
Phrenological head—on sideboard

Personal:

Briefcase   ⎫
Handkerchief ⎬ (Julian)

Off:

Chamois & 3 spoons (Butler)

Act I, Scene 3—Alice's Sitting Room

Hooded chair
Ottoman
Mirror

Act II, Scene 1—Library

Off R.:
Coffee service
Demitasse cups & saucers } (Butler)
Silver tray
Ring with keys
Liqueur bottle } (Julian)
Castle map

Act II, Scene 2—Library

On table:
Phrenological head } (Butler)
Old book

Act II, Scene 3—Alice's Sitting Room

Riding crop (Julian)

Act III—Library

Preset:
Champagne glasses (5) on tray—sideboard
Gun—drawer of sideboard
Off L.:
Fright wig } (Lawyer)
Briefcase
5 grey sheets } (Butler)
2 bottles of champagne

COSTUME PLOT

Act I—Scene 1

CARDINAL:
Red gown & sash & hat
Black shoes

LAWYER:
Grey business suit

Act I—Scene 2

JULIAN:
Cassock with clerical collar

LAWYER:
Same

BUTLER:
Butler's apron
Dark grey trousers
Black jacket
White shirt, black tie

Act I—Scene 3

JULIAN:
Same

BUTLER:
Same

LAWYER:
Same

ALICE:
Floor length afternoon gown, long sleeves,
Covered by:
Old lace shawl
Fur lap robe
Old lady mask
Fright wig
2 canes

Act II—Scene 1

JULIAN:
Same

BUTLER:
Same

LAWYER:
Black suit (or dinner clothes)

ALICE:
Evening gown

Act II—Scene 2

BUTLER:
Same

LAWYER:
Grey suit

Act II—Scene 3

JULIAN:
Same

ALICE:
Black lace negligee

Act III

JULIAN:
Black suit, regular shirt, black tie

BUTLER:
Same

LAWYER:
Black suit

CARDINAL:
Same

ALICE:
Traveling dress, with cloak to match

NEW PLAYS

• **MERE MORTALS by David Ives, author of** *All in the Timing.* Another critically acclaimed evening of one-act comedies combining wit, satire, hilarity and intellect -- a winning combination. The entire evening of plays can be performed by 3 men and 3 women. ISBN: 0-8222-1632-9

• **BALLAD OF YACHIYO by Philip Kan Gotanda.** A provocative play about innocence, passion and betrayal, set against the backdrop of a Hawaiian sugar plantation in the early 1900s. *"Gotanda's writing is superb ... a great deal of fine craftsmanship on display here, and much to enjoy."* --Variety. *"...one of the country's most consistently intriguing playwrights..."* --San Francisco Examiner. *"As he has in past plays, Gotanda defies expectations..."* --Oakland Tribune. [3M, 4W] ISBN: 0-8222-1547-0

• **MINUTES FROM THE BLUE ROUTE by Tom Donaghy.** While packing up a house, a family converges for a weekend of flaring tempers and shattered illusions. *"With MINUTES FROM THE BLUE ROUTE [Donaghy] succeeds not only in telling a story -- a typically American one with wide appeal, about how parents and kids struggle to understand each other and mostly fail -- but in notating it inventively, through wittily elliptical, crisscrossed speeches, and in making it carry a fairly vast amount of serious weight with surprising ease."* --Village Voice. [2M, 2W] ISBN: 0-8222-1608-6

• **SCAPIN by Molière, adapted by Bill Irwin and Mark O'Donnell.** This adaptation of Molière's 325-year-old farce, *Les Fourberies de Scapin,* keeps the play in period while adding a late Twentieth Century spin to the language and action. *"This SCAPIN, [with a] felicitous adaptation by Mark O'Donnell, would probably have gone over big with the same audience who first saw Molière's Fourberies de Scapin...in Paris in 1671."* --N.Y. Times. *"Commedia dell'arte and vaudeville have at least two things in common: baggy pants and Bill Irwin. All make for a natural fit in the celebrated clown's entirely unconventional adaptation."* --Variety [9M, 3W, flexible] ISBN: 0-8222-1603-5

• **THE TURN OF THE SCREW adapted for the stage by Jeffrey Hatcher from the story by Henry James.** The American master's classic tale of possession is given its most interesting "turn" yet: one woman plays the mansion's terrified governess while a single male actor plays everyone else. *"In his thoughtful adaptation of Henry James' spooky tale, Jeffrey Hatcher does away with the supernatural flummery, exchanging the story's balanced ambiguities about the nature of reality for a portrait of psychological vampirism..."* --Boston Globe. [1M, 1W] ISBN: 0-8222-1554-3

• **NEVILLE'S ISLAND by Tim Firth.** A middle management orientation exercise turns into an hilarious disaster when the team gets "shipwrecked" on an uninhabited island. *"NEVILLE'S ISLAND ... is that rare event: a genuinely good new play..., it's a comedic, adult LORD OF THE FLIES..."* --The Guardian. *"... A non-stop, whitewater deluge of comedy both sophisticated and slapstick.... Firth takes a perfect premise and shoots it to the extreme, flipping his fish out of water, watching them flop around a bit, and then masterminding the inevitable feeding frenzy."* --New Mexican. [4M] ISBN: 0-8222-1581-0

DRAMATISTS PLAY SERVICE, INC.
440 Park Avenue South, New York, NY 10016 212-683-8960 Fax 212-213-1539
postmaster@dramatists.com www.dramatists.com

NEW PLAYS

• **TAKING SIDES by Ronald Harwood.** Based on the true story of one of the world's greatest conductors whose wartime decision to remain in Germany brought him under the scrutiny of a U.S. Army determined to prove him a Nazi. *"A brave, wise and deeply moving play delineating the confrontation between culture, and power, between art and politics, between irresponsible freedom and responsible compromise."* --London Sunday Times. [4M, 3W] ISBN: 0-8222-1566-7

• **MISSING/KISSING by John Patrick Shanley.** Two biting short comedies, MISSING MARISA and KISSING CHRISTINE, by one of America's foremost dramatists and the Academy Award winning author of *Moonstruck.* *" ... Shanley has an unusual talent for situations ... and a sure gift for a kind of inner dialogue in which people talk their hearts as well as their minds...."* --N.Y. Post. MISSING MARISA [2M], KISSING CHRISTINE [1M, 2W] ISBN: 0-8222-1590-X

• **THE SISTERS ROSENSWEIG by Wendy Wasserstein, Pulitzer Prize-winning author of** *The Heidi Chronicles.* Winner of the 1993 Outer Critics Circle Award for Best Broadway Play. A captivating portrait of three disparate sisters reuniting after a lengthy separation on the eldest's 50th birthday. *"The laughter is all but continuous."* --New Yorker. *"Funny. Observant. A play with wit as well as acumen.... In dealing with social and cultural paradoxes, Ms. Wasserstein is, as always, the most astute of commentators."* --N.Y. Times. [4M, 4W] ISBN: 0-8222-1348-6

• **MASTER CLASS by Terrence McNally. Winner of the 1996 Tony Award for Best Play.** Only a year after winning the Tony Award for *Love! Valour! Compassion!,* Terrence McNally scores again with the most celebrated play of the year, an unforgettable portrait of Maria Callas, our century's greatest opera diva. *"One of the white-hot moments of contemporary theatre. A total triumph."* --N.Y. Post. *"Blazingly theatrical."* -- USA Today. [3M, 3W] ISBN: 0-8222-1521-7

• **DEALER'S CHOICE by Patrick Marber.** A weekly poker game pits a son addicted to gambling against his own father, who also has a problem but won't admit it. *" ... make tracks to DEALER'S CHOICE, Patrick Marber's wonderfully masculine, razor-sharp dissection of poker-as-life.... It's a play that comes out swinging and never lets up -- a witty, wisecracking drama that relentlessly probes the tortured souls of its six very distinctive ... characters. CHOICE is a cutthroat pleasure that you won't want to miss."* --Time Out (New York). [6M] ISBN: 0-8222-1616-7

• **RIFF RAFF by Laurence Fishburne.** RIFF RAFF marks the playwriting debut of one of Hollywood's most exciting and versatile actors. *"Mr. Fishburne is surprisingly and effectively understated, with scalding bubbles of anxiety breaking through the surface of a numbed calm."* --N.Y. Times. *"Fishburne has a talent and a quality...[he] possesses one of the vital requirements of a playwright -- a good ear for the things people say and the way they say them."* --N.Y. Post. [3M] ISBN: 0-8222-1545-4

DRAMATISTS PLAY SERVICE, INC.
440 Park Avenue South, New York, NY 10016 212-683-8960 Fax 212-213-1539
postmaster@dramatists.com www.dramatists.com